ROUSSEAU: THE LAST DAYS OF SPANISH NEW ORLEANS

With sketches of Spanish governors of Louisiana (1777-1803)
and glimpses of social life in New Orleans

I0134708

Raymond J. Martinez

Foreword by Jack D. L. Holmes

PELICAN PUBLISHING COMPANY
Gretna 2003

Copyright ©1964, 1975
By Raymond J. Martinez

First edition, 1964
Second edition, 1975
First Pelican edition, 2003

*The word "Pelican" and the depiction of a pelican are trademarks
of Pelican Publishing Company, Inc., and are registered in the
U.S. Patent and Trademark Office.*

Printed in the United States of America

Published by Pelican Publishing Company, Inc.
1000 Burmaster Street, Gretna, Louisiana 70053

Foreward

As the United States of America approached the 200th anniversary of its birth in 1976, numerous celebrations quickened the nation's interest in its history. Special books, reprints, and journal articles recall the sacrifices made by the Founding Fathers in launching our Ship of State. It is fitting, therefore, that this story of Pierre George Rousseau be told anew by Raymond J. Martinez, one of his lineal descendants. Perhaps it will remind Americans in general, and Louisianians in particular, that the American Revolution was not confined to the "13 Colonies" of the Atlantic Seaboard.

Historians are loath to change their attitudes, however, and a recent special issue of *American History Illustrated,* which was devoted to the American Revolution, did not even mention the Spanish campaigns against the British in Louisiana and West Florida during the war years, 1779-1781. How can historians ignore the fact that vital English, Loyalist and German reinforcements were diverted from the so-called "Southern Campaign" in the Carolinas by the efforts of Spanish regular and militia forces, Indians, blacks, and even a handful of Americans? Why is it so difficult to find in stories of the American Revolution the fascinating accounts of the siege and capture of Baton Rouge, Mobile and Pensacola? Are not these cities American, too?

My friend, Raymond J. Martinez, thinks they were and are. He follows the suggestion of Douglas Southall Freeman regarding the place of important men in history: preserve the records and tell the story sympathetically. To do this, he has drawn on records from Europe to America, published and unpublished. He has traced Rousseau's life from his birth at La Tremblade, France, June 3, 1751, through various stages. Although details on his early life before 1779 are sketchy, it appears that Rousseau was an officer in the young Continental Navy of the United States. It was natural, therefore, when a small detachment of Americans arrived in New Orleans

i

during 1779 that Rousseau was among them. This brings us the first phase of his remarkable career — the campaigns of Bernardo de Gálvez, 1779-1781.

Rousseau served as second mate to Captain William Pickles, who commanded an American privateer, the *Morris*. Pickles had originally been captain of an English vessel carrying cargo from London to the British settlements on the Mississippi River. When British corsairs captured Spanish vessels off the Gulf coast, Governor Bernardo de Gálvez retaliated by ordering several British ships confiscated. During 1777-1778, Pickles had the misfortune of seeing his vessel seized. Oliver Pollock, the American "angel" who spent his fortune helping both Spain and the United States during the Revolution, persuaded Gálvez and Pickles to wage naval warfare on British settlements and vessels on Lake Pontchartrain.

Mounting four 2½ pounders and one 1½ pounder, Pickles, Rousseau, Stephen Minor and Frederick and John Spell set forth in the *Morris* with British colors flying aloft. As the craft sighted the British ship *West Florida*, bound from Pensacola to Manchac on September 10, 1779, Pickles called to his fellow-officer aboard the British ship, Lieutenant John Payne. Pickles claimed to be carrying provisions from Pensacola, but as the two vessels came together, Pickles raised the American stripes "and at the same instant poured a volley of small arms into the vessel, by which the Lieutenant was killed and several of the men dangerously wounded."[1]

The initial naval success of an American privateer on Lake Pontchartrain proved very fortunate. The *Morris* fell victim to an early fall hurricane and lay on the bottom of the Mississippi. The captured British vessel *West Florida* was renamed the *Gálvez-Town*, in honor of the new settlement of Canary Island immigrants located on the Amite River, just below its confluence with Bayou Manchac.

Rousseau, who sustained three wounds as the first man who leaped aboard the British craft in its capture, won the steadfast support of Governor Gálvez, who recommended him for a breveted lieutenancy and command of the brigantine corsair *Gálvez-Town*. On January 1, 1780, Rousseau was named captain of militia. With $500 for additional armament, the *Gálvez-Town* cruised the lakes, capturing "contraband", which meant slaves and other property belonging to British and Loyalist settlers. Rousseau's name was soon as feared as that of James Willing, who had devastated lower Louisiana a few years earlier.

Gálvez next directed his attention at Mobile and its stout Fort Charlotte. Although he had a large convoy of landing barges, troop transports and land forces, Gálvez suffered again from the fickle whims of nature: a hurricane damaged many of his ships, and his most heavily-armed vessel, *El Volante,* ran aground on the bar guarding Mobile Bay. The only vessel remaining to assist the Spanish attack force was the *Gálvez-Town* under the command of Rousseau.

Still another hurricane prevented an immediate attack on the last British stronghold in the Gulf — Pensacola. The Spanish siege and capture of Pensacola may well have been her shining hour in Gulf Coast history. And part of the reason for the success of Spanish arms was the naval skill of Pierre George Rousseau. When the combined Spanish forces from the naval stronghold of Havana met with the tiny four-ship Louisiana Navy off Pensacola, there was a good deal of jocular exchange. Unfortunately for Spanish war aims, however, the kidding veiled a real dispute between the naval commander from Havana, Captain José Calbo de Irazabal, and the over-all commander of the expedition, Governor Bernardo de Gálvez of Louisiana.

The heavy-draft ships of the line under Calbo hesitated to expose themselves to grounding on the bars guarding the entrance to Pensacola's harbor. Navy men vs. army men: an old story, perhaps, but freshly demonstrated in 1781 at Pensacola. British cannon

III

fired heavy balls (28-pounders), which they believed guaranteed protection from an assault. But Pensacola has never been immune to attack, either from land or sea.

Thrice captured by opposing forces during the Franco-Spanish War, 1719-1722, it was vulnerable throughout its history. But, it did take courage to force its harbor entrance, and Rousseau commanded the small brigantine which did exactly that in 1781.

As the British cannon-balls fell harmlessly beside the craft, the flagship of Gálvez led the rest of Louisiana's tiny navy to refuge near the Spanish battery located on Sigüenza Point. In a festive *feu de joie,* Gálvez ordered a 15-gun salute from his cannon, which were loaded only with powder. Is it any wonder that a grateful monarch, Carlos III, granted Gálvez a coat-of-arms which showed the *Gálvez-Town* and the inscription, "YO SOLO" — I alone? It was another insult levelled by Gálvez against the timorous naval commanders of Havana.

With the fall of Pensacola Rousseau went to Jamaica, where he wrote to Gálvez's successor in New Orleans, Esteban Miró. A year later he received the rank of Captain of Infantry with the army salary, on January 15, 1784. There was an opening in the commandancy of the northwestern Louisiana post of Natchitoches, situated on the Red River. This post, founded in 1714, which is sometimes considered the oldest permanent settlement in the Louisiana Purchase (west of the Mississippi), had been the arena for such giants in Louisiana history as Louis Juchereau de St. Denis (the founder of St. Jean Baptiste in 1714) and Atanasio de Mézières, was hardly a challenge to the hyperactive Rousseau. To be stationed on the frontier with mundane chores was not his ideal of service. Rousseau served during 1786-1788, and when he quit it was to get married in New Orleans. "He acted," said Esteban Miró in 1792, "with behavior and discharged his duties to my entire satisfaction." This was typical of Rousseau — he invariably "discharged his duties" to the entire satisfaction of his superiors.

Considering that Rousseau was a skilled mariner, it is hardly surprising that he was named first commander of the Squadron of the Mississippi. The irony of this military unit was that it was a naval squadron only in the sense that it included ships. Its commanders and first mates were exclusively drawn from the ranks of the Louisiana *army* units—militia and regular army officers. A. P. Nasatir mentions Rousseau in his edited study of *Spanish War Vessels on the Mississippi*. What was the background of this unusual tactical weapon which kept the Mississippi Valley a Spanish area from the close of the American Revolution until almost the end of the century?

Gálvez considered the *Volante,* the frigate which ran aground at Mobile in 1780, one of the keys to defending New Orleans in 1777. During the late 1780's, Governor-general Esteban Miró agreed with the American double-agent, James Wilkinson, that Spain should create a strong, permanent squadron of galleys, galiots, bomber craft, and gunboats with which to protect the scattered Spanish posts from the Gulf to Upper Missouri.

In December, 1791, when the new governor-general, Baron de Carondelet, asked the governor of Natchez, Manuel Gayoso de Lemos, for his opinions concerning defense of the province, Gayoso wrote, "Floating forces are indispensable on this river, for without them the fortifications we have or may build will be much less effective." As a result of Gayoso's recommendations, Carondelet created the squadron and named Pierre George Rousseau as its first commander. His official patent is included in the Rare Louisiana material in the Kuntz Collection at Tulane University's archives.

What did Rousseau do with his little squadron, dominated as it was by career *army* officers? He guarded lower Louisiana against infiltration and attack by Jacobin agents and their American stooges during the

V

crises of 1793-1795. He cowed the pro-French Creole population of Lower Louisiana with the might of Spanish arms. He convoyed annual presents to the Indians of the Southeast, particularly at the Chickasaw Bluffs (present-day Memphis) and Nogales (present-day Vicksburg). He used the galleys to check descending craft and the occupants to see that unwelcome persons and seditious literature were not distributed in Spanish Louisiana. He used the galley squadron to transfer supplies, ammunition and troops from one post to another. Americans anxious to move against Spanish posts in Louisiana were forced to think twice before challenging Spain's squadron, which intended to keep the Mississippi a Spanish artery of commerce.

Mr. Martinez gives us the flavor of sailing on a galley in this squadron during the troubled days of 1793, when Citizen Edmont Genet was actively recruiting Americans for an attack on Spanish Louisiana. But in a larger sense, this 1793 mission was designed to locate a suitable post on the Mississippi where a fort might be constructed which would challenge effectively, the American or British ambitions of occupation. Rousseau selected the Chickasaw Bluffs, where Memphis, Tennessee, now stands.

While Spanish agents among the Chickasaws worked carefully to cement alliances which would lead to Chickasaw consent for a post to be built at the Bluffs, Rousseau reported to Natchez governor, Manuel Gayoso de Lemos. Together the two career officers journeyed north in 1795 and in late spring anchored on the Arkansas shore opposite the Chickasaw Bluffs. Within a few weeks, the trees had been cleared, and a fort begun. It was named San Fernando de las Barrancas in honor of the patron saint of the youthful prince, Fernando (Ferdinand) who was destined to become the last Spanish monarch before the independence of all Latin America—Ferdinand VII. Established through the joint cooperation of Rousseau and Gayoso, the fort gained legal foundation on June 20, wh n a group of Chickasaws signed the cession treaty for a small strip of territory near the Wolf River's confluence with the Mississippi. Among the signers was Pierre George Rousseau.

Illness struck Rousseau and he relinquished for a few years his command over the squadron to Manuel Garcîa. What forced him to return to duty, however, was the return from a Philippine prison to West Florida of the formidable leader of the war-like Seminoles, the ex-British officer and "adventurer," William Augustus Bowles. Bowles had captured the trading post of Panton, Leslie and Forbes located at San Marcos de Apalache in 1792, and his return to West Florida in 1799 boded evil for the Spanish control of the Indian trade. Sure enough, in 1800 Bowles and his Seminoles not only repeated their 1792 capture of the trading post, but this time succeeded in capturing the well-defended Fort San Marcos. Such a threat to Spanish honor and domination of the Indians deserved an answer.

Rousseau was induced to return from temporary retirement to take command of a ship in the squadron. The Spanish squadron launched a counter-attack under orders of Pensacola's governor, Vicente Folch y Juan. They succeeeded in driving Bowles and his allies from the fort and Bowles himself escaped by swimming across a snake-infested bayou. Rousseau's ships cruised along the Florida coast, hoping to intercept ships sailing from Nassau to West Florida with supplies, ammunition, and reinforcements for Bowles and his "State of Muskogee." The mutiny of the *Voltaire* occurred during this period when the ships were doing convoy and cruising duty between the capes of West Florida. Raymond Martinez transcribes the mutiny from the Spanish archives, which shows that duty in those days was little different from modern service as to tyranny, personal freedom, and individual rights.

Martinez does not seek to tell all there is to know about Rousseau. Rather, he seeks to create an impression, an image, a flavor. That he has done, without question. It is fortunate that one of Rousseau's descendants has such presence of mind, ability, and literary flair to shed additional light on Louisiana's unsung Revolutionary hero.

New Orleans, March, 1974

Jack D. L. Holmes

SOURCES

Caughey, John W. *Bernardo de Galvez in Louisiana, 1776-1783.* Berkeley: University of California Press, 1934. Reprinted, Gretna, Louisiana: Pelican, 1972.

Claiborne, John Francis Hamtramck. *Mississippi as a Province, Territory and State.* Jackson: Barksdale, 1880. Reprint edition, Baton Rouge: Louisiana State University Press, 1964.

Fortier, Alcee. *A History of Louisiana.* 4 vols. Paris and New York: Goupil & Co., and Manzi, Joyant & Co., 1904.

Gayarre, Charles Etienne Arthur. *History of Louisiana, The Spanish Domination.* New York: Redfield, 1854.

Holmes, Jack D. L. (ed.). *Documentos inéditos para la historia de la Luisiana, 1792-1810.* Vol. XV. *Colección Chilmalistac* (Madrid: Ediciones José Porrúa Turanzas, 1963.

_____, *Gayoso, the Life of A Spanish Governor in the Mississippi Valley, 1789-1799.* Baton Rouge: Louisiana State University Press for the Louisiana Historical Association, 1965. Reprint edition, Gloucester, Mass.: Peter Smith, 1968.

_____, *Honor and Fidelity, the Louisiana Infantry Regiment and the Louisiana Militia Companies, 1766 1821.* Birmingham: Louisiana Collection Series, 1965.

_____, (ed.). "Louisiana in 1795, the Earliest Extant Issue of the *Moniteur de la Louisiane." Louisiana History,* VII, No. 2 (Spring, 1966), 133-151.

_____, "Spanish-American Rivalry Over the Chickasaw Bluffs, 1780-1795, East Tennessee Historial Society *Publications,* No. 34 (1962), 26-57.

Kinnaird, Lawrence. "The Significance of William Augustus Bowles' Seizure of Panton's Apalachee Store in 1792." *Florida Historical Quarterly,* IX (1931), 156-192.

_____, (ed.). *Spain in The Mississippi Valley, 1765-1794.* 3 Parts. Vols. II-IV, American Historical Association *Annual Report For* 1945. Washington: Government Printing Office, 1946-1949.

McAlister, Lyle N. (ed.). "The Marine Forces of William Augustus Bowles and His 'State of Muskogee'." *Florida Historical Quarterly,* XXXII, No. 1 (July, 1953), 3-27.

Nasatir, Abraham P. (ed.). *Spanish War Vessels on the Mississippi, 1792-1796.* New Haven and London: Yale University Press, 1968.

Whitaker, Arthur Preston. *The Mississippi Question, 1795-1803.* New York: D. Appleton-Century, 1934.

PIERRE GEORGE ROUSSEAU

Preface

This book is an effort to record as accurately as possible the career of an able officer of the American Revolution and the Spanish military force during the Spanish regime in Louisiana, Missouri, and West Florida. The achievements of Pierre George Rousseau are mentioned frequently but briefly in various publications and in the records of archives of Spain, France, and America. They all testify to his skill as a soldier, his reliability as an agent in diplomatic missions, and his eminently fine judgment in handling the difficult situations with which he was often confronted. Only a man of remarkable ability and extraordinary self-command could have held the important post of commanding general of the galleys of the Mississippi under all six Spanish governors of Louisiana from Galvez to Salcedo, during whose administration Louisiana was transferred to the United States (December 20, 1803), always maintaining the confidence and high respect of them all.

Though this work, owing to the scattered records, has required years of research, I cannot say that it has been an arduous task, for the subject has been extremely interesting. And in the quest for information I have very pleasantly made the acquaintance of many students of history and genealogy. Among those to whom I am deeply indebted for information and advice are: Miss Elizabeth C. Rousseau of Washington, D.C., who contributed much valuable information; John Alf. Rousseau of New Orleans (a great-great-grandson of Pierre George Rousseau); Mrs. Herbert C. Parker of New Orleans (who is related to the General through his wife, Catherine Wiltz Milhet); Charles L. Dufour of New Orleans; Mrs. Alden McLellan of New Orleans; Mrs. Edwin X. deVerges of New Orleans; Col. Wilfred E. Lessard of Baton Rouge, La.; Miss Helen Arnoult of New Orleans; Robert G. Polack of New Orleans; Sidney L. Villere of New Orleans; Stanley Faye of Aurora, Ill.; Louis R. Nardini of Natchitoches, La.; Leo R. Wertheimer of New Orleans; Madame Helene Forgit-

Rousseau of La Tremblade, France; Mrs. Dugue Bendernagel of New Orleans; Dr. Thomas H. Gandy of Natchez, Mississippi; Mrs. Edouard F. (Ann) Henriques, Jr., of New Orleans, who drew the maps and other illustrations in this volume, and I am especially indebted to Mrs. Mary C. Easterling and her grandson, Major Thomas Harrison Rousseau, who provided valuable information for this book.

_____

Rousseau Meets Galvez.
The Beginning of a Long Friendship

Bernardo de Galvez had been governor of Louisiana but a short time when he met a young officer of the Continental navy, Pierre George Rousseau, who was to become his steadfast friend, and who was also to render a great service to him and all the succeeding Spanish governors of the colony. In order to evaluate the accomplishments of this man, and to learn of the high esteem in which he was held by the Spanish governors of Louisiana and the Court of Spain, it is necessary to read the letters and reports of the various officials of the Spanish regime, many of which have been gathered from the archives of Seville, and published by the American Historical Association (especially in the volume entitled *Spain in the Mississippi Valley*). Many records concerning his military career were found among papers in the Library of Congress, heretofore untranslated from the Spanish and unpublished.

This information was within the reach of former writers of Louisiana history but it was not easily available and many of his achievements in diplomacy and military are imperfectly known.

A striking example is the case of the capture of Pensacola, an expedition which was organized with his assistance and advice, for he had made himself thoroughly familiar with the area in which the fleet for the attack was to proceed. He had sounded the channel and surveyed the territory. He led the way, for he commanded the Galvez-Town with Galvez at his side. And yet some eminent historians have ignored him. It was in appreciation of this splendid expedition that the King of Spain requested Galvez to place on his coat of arms YO SOLO (I alone). This was true, for the Cuban fleet refused to join in the attack and capture of Pensacola. (See page 20.)

The Spanish governors and their officers have been quite fair to him. It is from their letters and reports

5

Don Bernardo de Galvez

that we must form an estimate of his career as a soldier in Louisiana.

As the historians of Louisiana, with few exceptions, have been neglectful of Rousseau, they have been in a sense unfair to Galvez, for they have given the impression that he was willing to accept all the offices, military promotions, and honors conferred upon him without even a passing mention of his "best friend," who helped him achieve glory. There is an abundance of evidence, heretofore unpublished, that Galvez himself was very grateful to Rousseau, and accorded him full credit for his loyalty and assistance.

The following are excerpts from the account of "Don Pedro Rousseau," written by Henry C. Castellanos, and published in the Times-Democrat on September 8, 1895, showing that Galvez was never reluctant to acknowledge the valuable services that Rousseau rendered him, and that, in fact, he was always prompt in praising him to his superiors in the Spanish Court.

A Newspaper's Account

Henry C. Castellanos, in his article, THE SIEGE OF PENSACOLA and THE STORY OF PIERRE ROUS-SEAU, published in the Times-Democrat, September 8, 1895, gives a glowing account of Rousseau's skill and daring. He said it "was on the 17th of March, 1781," that in the vicinity of Pensacola, which was well forti-fied, there stood a "large Spanish fleet, consisting of one formidable ship of the line, two frigates and a number of armed transports apparently afraid to ven-ture within the narrow entrance that led to the port. A little beyond it, securely anchored, was to be seen a small brig accompanied by two gunboats, which consti-tuted the little navy of Louisiana. Beyond and before loomed up the sandy waters of Santa de Rosa, covered with moving and excited battalions of Spanish infantry and artillery, while on the right, a fortress, bristling with cannon and red-coated veterans, seemed to invite attack and frown contemptuously upon the invading forces. At about 3 o'clock in the afternoon a boat was seen leaving the island and directing its course toward the brig. It contained several officers in gaudy uniforms, among whom was distinguished a young man clad in the costume of a General. His bearing was haughty and his step elastic as he nimbly sprang over the railings of the vessel and appeared before her commander. The craft was the Galvez-Town, her captain Pierre George Rousseau (an officer of the Continental navy), and the visitor, Galvez himself.

" 'Captain,' said the latter, 'I have come to place my honor and that of Spain into your hands. The fleet refuses to follow me through this perilous passage. Will you convey me and staff to the attack?'

" 'My General,' replied the bluff, honest and fear-less sea dog, 'my life and ship are yours to dispose of.' 'Then let us hoist sail at once, and show these cursed English what Spaniards can do.' "

"And hardly had these words escaped his lips," said Castellanos, "than the drum beat called the men to arms, and Rousseau directing the pilot at the wheel led the way, with the broad pennant of Castile and Leon flaunting in the air, notwithstanding the shower of bullets and missiles which were tearing the canvas to shreds." The English were stupefied with wonder at this act of audacity but much more amazed was Galvez who watched his enterprise succeed beyond his expectations. "An unpretentious but fearless Captain," said Castellanos, "had displayed greater judgement than Galvez and all his officers combined."

Although the Continental Congress had previously made plans to drive the British out of Florida (even before Spain declared war on England), and Rousseau was still an officer in the American navy, with instructions to aid Galvez in the capture of Pensacola, there is no record available to show that he received any special recognition from that source as a result of his unusual feat. But, as Castellanos says, "such a service demanded recognition, and Galvez, who was just, loyal and grateful in his appreciation of those whose good fortune it was to serve under him, rendered a faithful account of the affair to his uncle, Joseph Galvez, who was then occupying in Madrid the post of President of the Council of the Indies, and was the confidential Minister of the King."

Rousseau received the following letter:

In consequence of the information furnished by Don Bernardo de Galvez, Lieutenant General of our royal armies and Governor of Louisiana, the King has been apprised of the zeal, noted bravery and distinguished conduct which have characterized your course in his royal service from the period that the General placed you in command of the brig named "Galvez-Town" at the beginning of the war now being waged against Great Britain. This information has caused great pleasure to his majesty, in whose royal name he bids me tender your worship his most sincere thanks (a duty which I am now performing) and advise you at the same time that his royal beneficence will not overlook the meritorius deeds performed by you in the discharge of the various duties to which you were assigned. This communication I forwarded to your notice for your own satisfaction. May God preserve your worship many years.

San Ildefonso on the 18th of August, 1781

Jph. de Galvez

Galvez was in every sense a gentleman, and when the King conferred honors upon him for having "forced his way *alone* through the harbor of Pensacola" he wrote Rousseau the following letter:

> Among the distinguished honors with which the King, our Master, has been pleased to manifest his appreciation of my humble services, he has deemed proper to notice particularly the forcing of my way alone through the harbor of Pensacola, assisted only by the brig "Gavez-Town." I owe to his sovereign indulgence (that my posterity may hold this action of mine in perpetual memory) the special privilege of inscribing the aforesaid brig "Galvez-Town" on my coat of arms and the motto "Yo Solo." . . . (I alone).

> And inasmuch as my wishes would remain ungratified, were I to omit the recognition in the officers of my said brig, of the valor, intelligence and resolution displayed in that case of emergency, I desire for this reason that your worships, Monsieur Rousseau, as the first, and Monsieur Duparc, as the second, of the parties to whom I am more particularly indebted for the success of that undertaking, I desire, I say, to give you both together with a copy of royal grant and this letter of thanks, a public testimonial; expecting that in the meantime the King as he has promised, shall reward you in a more worthy and authentic form.

> May Our Lord preserve your worships many years.

> Guarico, 15th. of April, 1782

> Bernardo de Galvez

To Senor Don Pedro Rousseau

Charles III always kept his promise, and Rousseau was promoted to a Lieutenant Colonelcy in the line, and assigned to the command of the Spanish fleet operating on the Mississippi, Lake Pontchartrain, and the West Florida coast. This force consisted mainly of brigs, schooners, armed galleys and gunboats. It was a formidable fleet and kept the surrounding waters free of intruders.

9

Charles III of Spain to whom Louisiana was ceded by Louis XV of France in 1762. He instructed Bernardo de Galvez to give aid to George Washington during the American Revolution.

Charles III, Most Methodical Man in Europe

Charles III was a man of good sense, and always grateful for the achievements of his magistrates, whom he selected from the best educated and most able citizens of his realm. He was the son of Philip V and Elizabeth Farnese. As a young soldier he had not won much glory but had learned to discipline himself, a habit which he retained for the rest of his life. He was the most methodical man in his kingdom. In his habit of living he was as regular as the clock itself. Every Spaniard knew (exactly the hour) when the King would go to bed, and when he would arise; and the exact day he would undertake a particular journey it was his custom to make. He was like a human almanac indicating the rising and setting of the sun, and the changing of the seasons. From the first of January to the thirty-first of December the exact hour of every occupation and every social event to occur was set down and minutely observed. His private life was that of a Christian gentleman. Although a Bourbon he had none of the vices of that family, and being highly intelligent, notwithstanding his idiosyncrasies, he restored prosperity to Spain.

10

Young Galvez Was An Able Administrator

Bernardo de Galvez was sworn in as governor-general of Louisiana Jan. 1, 1777. He succeeded Luis de Unzaga who, following Alexander O'Reilly, had endeared himself to the people of New Orleans by his easy-going administration. Galvez had married a native of the city, Felicites, the daughter of Sieur Gilbert Antoine St. de Maxent, and was reluctant to leave but the Spanish government had appointed him Captain General of Caracas, and he had no choice. Galvez was only twenty-one years old but his uncle, Joseph de Galvez, was one of the most powerful nobles in Spain. He was Secretary of State and President of Council of the Indies. Galvez' Father, Don Matias de Galvez, was Presidente of Guatemala.

When he became governor of Louisiana he was authorized to communicate directly with his uncle, who was very fond of him, and therefore his power in administering the affairs of the colony was almost unlimited. But he never abused his privileges and authority. His letters to his uncle are very serious and they reveal that this man in his thirties was fully aware of his responsibilities, that he was realistic, and not in the least confused concerning his main objective, which was to make the colony a profitable connection for Spain. He took measures to introduce the cultivation of hemp and flax at the suggestion of his uncle, but realizing that he knew little about the agricultural possibilities of the country he consulted Francisco Cruzat, whom he did not particularly like, and was advised that that was not a good crop for this country. The objections were that the soil was not suitable for these products — which was not entirely correct—that the inhabitants did not have the money to buy seed nor to buy slaves, which he felt was necessary in order to produce considerable quantities. Cruzat referred to the "weakness" of the population, by which he meant the scarcity of money and labor. They grew very little hemp and flax. The people of the lower Mississippi region grew indigo, one of their crops. But the inhabitants of the Illinois country planted wheat and the yields were abundant.

Family Background of Pierre George Rousseau

Pierre George Rousseau was born at La Tremblade, in the province of Saintonge, France. On a page of the old Parish records kept prior to the French Revolution by the Church at La Tremblade there is written: PIERRE-GEORGES, son of Sieur Pierre Rousseau (Marine Captain) and of Marie Eustelle Daniaud, born and baptized on June 3, 1751. He came of an old Huguenot family who had lived for generations in that area, a Huguenot stronghold since before the Edict of Nantes (1598). His ancestors were followers of Louis II de Bourbon, Prince de Condé—civil reformer. In addition to the family seat in La Tremblade, the family owned an estate in southern France, at Arles. But Pierre George's father made his headquarters in the arcaded city of La Rochelle, for he was captain of a merchant ship which he owned, and which plied regularly between this ancient, seafaring city and American ports along the Atlantic coast. The Captain put in frequently at Charlestown, South Carolina, where at one time some of his relatives were living; among them Hilaire and James Rousseau. Hilaire was the son of Theodore Rousseau, a Huguenot immigrant who came to this country on the ship "Peter and Anthony", landing at Jamestown, Virginia, in 1701-2. Hilaire settled in Stafford County, Virginia. His son, James, married Lucy Harrison, daughter of Benjamin Harrison of Berkeley, Virginia, and their son, David, was the father of General Lovell H. Rousseau, statesman and soldier. The Rousseau family had been long established in this country and had become influential.

Pierre George Rousseau's mother died when he was quite young and his father, Captain Rousseau, brought his sons to America. There is no positive record of where the Captain settled when he first came to this country with his very young children but according to family tradition he resided for a while among relatives in Virginia or South Carolina. At least he did not remain long on the Atlantic coast, for Pierre George states when called upon to testify in the famous Louisiana

"Batture Controversy" case in 1807 that he was a resident of New Orleans in 1764. This was, he said, the first time he came to this country — no doubt meaning Louisiana. Newspaper accounts at the time of Pierre George Rousseau's death in 1810 state that he came to America as "a mere infant." Certainly he was no "mere infant" in 1764. And there is little doubt that he was educated in an English colony, for English was as familiar to him as his native tongue.

In 1779 Pierre George Rousseau was ordered by George Washington to report at New Orleans to assist Bernardo de Galvez, the governor of Louisiana, in routing the British from the Gulf of Mexico; from Lake Pontchartrain to West Florida. He played a decisive role in the capture of the *West Florida*.

The Capture of The West Florida

His first adventure of note (or of which we have a definite record) occurred while he was second in command on the MORRIS, a frigate of the Continental navy operating on Lake Pontchartrain. This vessel, which was commanded by Captain William Pickles, set out in 1779, at the request of Galvez, to capture an English vessel, the WEST FLORIDA, which was causing considerable trouble to coastwise and overseas shipping. The British stubbornly defended their ship, which was well armed, and in this engagement, which cost the lives of six men, Rousseau displayed great courage. The fire of the British did not deter him; he steered the Morris up against the West Florida and personally led his men aboard for a hand-to-hand battle. He was severely wounded but continued fighting until the enemy surrendered. There is no clear record of what Captain Pickles did during this engagement. For some reason, unknown, he did not mention Rousseau in his report. He took full credit, however, for the capture of the WEST FLORIDA. But Galvez, in a letter dated April 29, 1783, states clearly that Rousseau captured the WEST FLORIDA, and does not mention Pickles. Rousseau himself stated in his petition for a pension (after the Louisiana Purchase) addressed to the King of Spain, with documents of proof attached, that he captured the WEST FLORIDA. Neither does *he* mention Captain Pickles.

There are, therefore, conflicting statements as to who captured and commanded the WEST FLORIDA. Charles Oscar Paulin in his book, THE NAVY OF THE AMERICAN REVOLUTION, gives Captain Pickles credit for the capture of the vessel, and also states that it was later under his command, and cruised on Lake Pontchartrain, at the request of Galvez, for protection of the trade. But the Continental Congress made it evident to Oliver Pollock (commercial agent at New Orleans during the Revolution) that the government wished the naval forces on the Mississippi to proceed to Philadelphia. Oliver Pollock gave Captain Pickles orders, therefore, to sail for Philadelphia (January 20, 1780), after taking on a cargo of tafia and sugar at Havana. He directed Captain Pickles to join the fleet of Galvez before making the trip to Philadelphia and help him in the reduction of Mobile and Pensacola. Pickles probably obeyed orders (if this is not an error in reporting events) and if he did, his ship, the WEST FLORIDA, took part in the siege of Pensacola. Eventually, it is stated, Captain Pickles picked up the tafia and sugar at Havana, and steered the WEST FLORIDA to Philadelphia, were she was judged unsuitable for navigation and sold.

The papers of the GENERAL ARCHIVES OF THE INDIES and letters written by Galvez give Rousseau full credit for the capture of the WEST FLORIDA, and state also that he was in actual command of the vessel. This is a strange incident in reporting events. Paulin says that "after aiding the capture of Mobile and taking a small prize . . . the WEST FLORIDA proceeded to Philadelphia, where she arrived about the first of June, 1780." Certainly she did not then take part in the "reduction" of Pensacola, for that did not occur until in March of 1781.

A Map of Lake Pontchartrain showing where the Battle
of the Morris and the West Florida was fought

15

A Story Handed Down

There is no clear record of the vessel to which Pierre George Rousseau was attached or which he commanded before he was transferred to the Morris of the Continental Navy operating on Lake Pontchartrain. But there can be little doubt that he was in charge of a frigate (or some type of vessel) on the Atlantic coast around 1778, for the following account of one of his interesting experiences handed down through generations of his family cannot be mere fiction. It may have been slightly changed in the telling but it is basically true.

He was in command of a frigate (nobody remembered its name) sailing along the coast of South Carolina. The weather was stormy and the visibility poor. He spied a merchant vessel which was approaching his at a good speed. Fearing that it was an enemy ship, he instructed his crier to take the megaphone and yell "A-hoy, what ship is that and who is in command?" The reply came quickly. "This is an American ship and Nicholas Rousseau is in command. Who is your commander?" Pierre then took the megaphone himself and replied: "It is I, Pierre, your brother. Stay close; the storm is increasing; we may have to rescue you." There was a moment of silence. Then Nicholas took his megaphone and cried out: "Indeed, we are good sailors; you'd better look after yourself." . . . "Ha, ha," cried Pierre, "the wind and the waves do not know you, except as a speck on the ocean. Pull up along-side of this ship; it is sound, and its commander knows his business." . . . "Bosh," said Nicholas, "I taught you what you know, and that isn't much."

The velocity of the wind increased, and by the flashes of lightning Pierre could see the mountainous waves sweeping over the little merchant ship. He then steered his frigate along-side of it and made ready to rescue his brother and the ship's crew. But as if by a wave of the hand of the Lord the wind suddenly shifted, and in a moment the sea was calm.

"Sail on," cried Nicholas, "your ship is safe."

Ordering his men to pull the frigate alongside the merchant ship, Pierre called out to his brother, "you ungrateful, cold-blooded wretch, I was ready to save you and your crew, and the least you can do is to invite me to a cup of coffee."

Nicholas, when his vessel had been moored up against the frigate, called to Pierre, "come aboard, I'll give you coffee and brandy . . ."

"Coffee," said Pierre; "I don't drink brandy."

"Truly," said Nicholas, "you are too young."

Pierre George boarded the ship and embraced his brother whom he had not seen in several years. They had a meal together and then parted. They did not meet again until long after the end of the American Revolution, in which they were both engaged.

Rousseau with Galvez in the Capture of Mobile, Baton Rouge, Natchez, Manchac and Pensacola

As Galvez expected, Spain declared war against Great Britain on May 8, 1779, and he was authorized to take part in the American Revolution. He first advanced the colonists, through their agent at New Orleans, Oliver Pollock, a large sum of money (around seventy thousand dollars) to buy arms and ammunitions. He then organized an expedition for the capture of Baton Rouge, Natchez, and Fort Manchac. Leaving New Orleans on August 27, 1779, with Rousseau as one of his lieutenants, he proceeded up the Mississippi. He had a small fleet composed of one schooner and three gunboats, and an army of 1430 men, including militiamen, eighty free men of color, recruits and 160 Indians. His fleet though small was formidable. He captured Manchac on the way, and arrived at Baton Rouge on September 7. On September 21 the English surrendered the fort at Baton Rouge, and also the fort at Natchez.

After the capture of these towns on the Mississippi he undertook the capture of Mobile, and Rousseau, still an officer of the Continental navy, gave him able assistance. The expedition left New Orleans on February 5, 1780, and on the 14th of March compelled the English, under Elias Durnford, to surrender. The last stronghold then in the hands of the British in West Florida was Pensacola. Galvez returned to New Orleans and made preparations for the capture of that place during the following year. In this expedition he gave Rousseau a leading part, for he had been impressed with his military skill during the previous campaigns on the river.

An Authentic Account of The Siege of Pensacola

Journalists who report events and men who write history are always under great temptation to endow their subject-heroes with unusual qualities and place them in dramatic situations. This is often necessary to produce a good story. But as a result there are conflicting accounts of nearly every heroic figure of history. There is no doubt that Pierre George Rousseau was one of the outstanding heroes in the siege of Pensacola but there are many different stories concerning his adventures. One traditional account handed down by his family is that in preparation for the siege he disguised himself as a fisherman, and in an open boat travelled the channel leading to Pensacola, and made an excellent map of the area, which he was well able to do, for he was skilled in civil engineering. Thus when he returned to the Galvez-Town, which he commanded, and on which Galvez was stationed, he had a very accurate outline of the territory ahead, and knew exactly the strength of the British fortifications. There is another account in which it is stated that he left his fleet and embarked in an open boat to sound the channel in order to make certain that his ship could sail through. When he returned he said that "the heaviest ship in the fleet with the heaviest load can navigate the channel," that he would lead the way, and others could follow.

Nearly everybody in New Orleans familiar with his history has a slightly different story but they all have a basis of truth. This is the most plausible account:

Pedro Rousseau (as the Spaniards called him — the French called him Pierre, and the Anglo-Saxons called him Peter) sounded the channel leading to Pensacola. This was done before the fleet was ready to sail. It was, in fact, shortly after he and Galvez had captured Baton Rouge, Manchac and Natchez, and had, therefor driven the English forces out of West Florida. Then ober 16, 1780, they went to Havana to procure reinforcements, for that was the headquarters for Spain in the Americas, but on the return trip some of their transports vanished in a terrible storm. Galvez went back to Havana, says Judge Martin in his History of Louisiana, and "sailed again (to capture Pensacola) on February 28, 1781, with a man-of-war, two frigates, and several transports, on board of which were fourteen hundred and fifteen soldiers, a competent train of artillery and abundance of ammunition. The fleet was commanded by Don Josef Calbo de Irazabal."

Judge Martin gives the impression that Irazabal commanded Galvez' fleet, which is not correct. Irazabal commanded his own fleet from Havana, and Rousseau commanded Galvez's fleet, the flagship of which was the Galvez-Town. But when Galvez asked Irazabal to cross the bar he refused. He was then advised that Rousseau had sounded the channel and found it to be deep enough for the fleet to sail through. He still refused.

GALVEZ SENDS A MESSAGE TO DON JOSEF SOLANO, COMMANDER OF THE CUBAN FLEET, URGING HIM TO JOIN HIM IN THE ATTACK. SOLANO IS INSULTED, AND REFUSES

The officers of the Cuban fleet were not directly under Galvez and were accountable only to the government of Spain.

But one wonders what happened to Irazabal when reading the account of the seige of Pensacola from Vicente Davila, ed., Archivo del General Miranda (Caracas, 15 v to 1933) tomo 1, Viajes, 1750-1785, it is learned that Galvez and Rousseau of the brig Galvez-Town, "sent an officer, Gelabert, an engineer, in a boat to the vessel of the (Cuban) Squadron Commander, Don Josef Solano, to report that a 32-pounder ball picked up in camp, which he brought with him and presented, was of those that the fort at the entrance had fired. He said that he who had the honor and courage should follow him, for he himself was going on the Galvez-Town with Galvez and Rousseau to prove the safety of the passage." This message (from Galvez) was delivered

THE GALVEZ-TOWN LEADS THE WAY TO THE
CAPTURE OF PENSACOLA

GULF COAST CAMPAIGNS OF GALVEZ

by word of mouth on the poopdeck in the presence of the crew.

"Don Josef Solano in reply told Gelabert that his general (Galvez) was an audacious lowlife, a traitor to the King and to the country, and that the insult he had just given to his person and to all the officers of the navy he would carry to the feet of the King, that he was a coward who 'tenia los Canones por la Culata,' and that any other similar oral message should be sent to him by a person unworthy of consideration, and not by an officer, so that he might have the pleasure of hanging him from the yardarm. The commandant had called all the officers of the ship to the poopdeck so that they may hear his reply."

Galvez and Rousseau were not upset by this undignified reply which Gelabert brought back to them. They thought it ludicrous. At four o'clock in the afternoon Rousseau entered the channel with the brig **Galvez-Town**, accompanied by three armed sloops, and **went** through despite the firing of 28 cannons from the fort. This unexpected demonstration, says the report, "stimulated (the bravery of) the captains of Solano's frigate, who presented themselves, asking permission to enter, to which Solano did not consent but gave a general order forbidding any movement of the vessels from their anchorage." It should be explained, however, that Solano had previously tried to take his convoy into the bay but that his ship-of-the-line ran aground. It seemed questionable to him, therefore, whether the brigs and frigate should attempt to enter.

"But at 8 P.M. of the same day a colonel sent by Galvez arrived at Solano's vessel to pacify him. He explained that Galvez meant only to exhort him, not to insult. This explanation satisfied Solano, and he ordered the convoys to enter the port at 2 o'clock on the afternoon of the next day, which was the 19th of March. They anchored without injury, notwithstanding the 140 cannonades that the fort made against them."

"Four days later (March 23) Galvez sent word to Solano that he would have lunch with him on the next day, and that for his part he would give orders to the army officers that they maintain perpetual silence concerning the matters of the past. But this luncheon engagement was cancelled, for the wind was high the next morning and Solano set sail for Havana to get reinforcements. He returned on April 21, and the next day passed the Barrancas fort. The journal of an officer of his ship says that: 'Upon our passage before the aforesaid batteries the enemy fired at us 14 cannonades of large caliber, well aimed. As it happened, none touched the boat. We see, however, two reasons why this fire did no harm among so many boats as passed on this occasion: The first is that the distance where our boats usually pass is greater than it appears to be on water level (in my opinion it is more than 700 toesas). The other is that the battery being considerably in domination, the fire is, as a result, *fixante,* and consequently very uncertain.' (Tiro fiante is applied to fire that is made directly upon an object)." Apparently this officer made a close estimate of the distance between the cannons and the boats, for it was later found to be 730 toesas. A toesa is 6 Spanish feet; 5½ English feet.

The Spanish fleet landed on April 22, and established camps before the city of Pensacola. General Campbell, in charge of the British forces, led an assault against the camps, killed many Spanish soldiers, and destroyed a considerable amount of arms and amunition. But the army of Galvez advanced upon the city and blew up the main powder magazine of Fort George. The explosion rocked the city of Pensacola from one end to the other. This opened a passage, and on May 9, 1781 Galvez marched into the city of Pensacola, compelling the British to capitulate. Under the white flag General Campbell stated his terms of surrender: that the British troops be conveyed in Spanish ships to a British port. Otherwise he would fight to the last man. Galvez demurred but finally agreed. Perhaps he did not wish to see men slaughtered unnecessarily, for his army in men and equipment was vastly superior to that of General Campbell. But Galvez committed a serious

23

error, he permitted the British troops to be taken to Brooklyn, where upon their arrival the Continental army was not in a position to hold them as prisoners of war, and they were set free or served to augment the British forces. This greatly displeased George Washington but he was apparently satisfied when Galvez wrote him a letter of explanation. Irrespective of the terms, which could have been more favorable to Galvez, by this capitulation the province of West Florida was acquired by Spain. Although the troops fared well, the terms were extremely severe for the British citizens. (Refer to the chapter on Panton, Leslie & Co.)

The accounts of Rousseau's courtship and social activities as related in the following pages are handed down by tradition. Having been repeated many times by members of succeeding generations, perhaps each time in a slightly different way, there may be some variance in names, places, and incidents but they are basically true.

A Glance at Social Life in New Orleans
After the Revolution

Following the capture of Pensacola Galvez and Rousseau returned to New Orleans for a rest. Galvez retired to his country estate, El Guarico, in St. Bernard parish on a beautiful spot in the midst of oak trees along the Mississippi River. Rousseau remained aboard the Galvez-Town, which was anchored opposite the Place d'Armes, for that was his ship, Galvez told him, as long as he wished to command it. But he frequently went to El Guarico, where he was lavishly entertained, and where he met members of the families with such names as Crozat, Dreux, Conti, St. Maxent, Wiltz, Garic, Poey-farre, de la Chaise, Daunoy, Marigny, Almonester, de Kernion, Villere, Forstall, Dufossat, de la Pena, Milhet, and others.

On an evening when he was there he asked Galvez to walk out and talk with him under a huge oak tree that stood in the yard. "I have something which I should like to discuss privately," he said.

"Then," said Galvez, "we'll sit on the bench under the tree; that is where I often sit to ponder over things."

When they were comfortably seated Rousseau said, "I am, as you know, attached to the Continental navy, and am perhaps needed on the Atlantic coast."

"You are needed here," said Galvez, "for if the English can again control the Floridas they will be troublesome to the American cause."

"I should prefer to stay with you," said Rousseau, "but that must be with the knowledge and consent of the Continental Congress."

"Don't let that concern you," replied Galvez. "You are a man of honor, I know, but Oliver Pollock, who is the accredited agent for the Continental Congress, has been advised and has approved."

"I know," said Rousseau, "that his advice is always accepted."

"You have now explained yourself," said Galvez. "But I have something in mind. This man, Cornwallis,

A VIEW OF NEW ORLEANS IN 1803

cannot hold out long; the fighting will soon be over. I wish you to remain in the Spanish service as commanding general of the galleys of the Mississippi, for no man knows the territory so well, and who at the same time is so capable a warrior."

"Thank you," said Rousseau. "I appreciate the compliment, and shall be glad to serve in that capacity."

This conversation took place in the summer of 1781, and General Cornwallis surrendered in October of the same year. The Treaty of Paris (1783) formally recognized the United States as a nation, and at the same time England formally returned West Florida to Spain.

To the Continental navy Rousseau was only one of many officers. His name appeared without comment in a list of officers furnished the United States Congress. But to Galvez and his soldiers he was a young navy officer who had won fame, and upon whom they could depend, for he had proved himself able and courageous. After his appointment as commanding general of the galleys of the Mississippi he was constantly consulted concerning the defense of the colony.

There was much gayety in the social life of New Orleans during this period, for the French, though unpleasant or tragic incidents caused by Ulloa and O'Reilly were fresh in their memory, had accepted the Spaniards socially as well as officially. Margarethe Wiltz Milhet had married Major Jacinto Panis, who served under O'Reilly and also under Galvez. She was the widow of Joseph Milhet who was shot in the Place d'Armes with other leaders of the colony who had objected to Spanish rule. Major Panis, it so happened, was the officer who gave the order to fire. But he was acting for O'Reilly, and had no choice in the matter. Several years later he had "implored the King's permission to marry Margarethe Wiltz, widow of Joseph Milhet." It was said that Margarethe never knew that Panis had been the officer who gave the order to fire, for she was happy in her second marriage and nobody would ever dare tell her.

GALVEZ AND ROUSSEAU BOTH MARRY
NEW ORLEANS GIRLS

Galvez himself during this period met an attractive young lady, Felicie de St. Maxent d'Estrehan, widow of Jean Baptiste Honore d'Estrehan, daughter of Sieur Gilbert Antoine St. de Maxent*, and after a brief courtship they were married. She was the sister of Unzaga's wife, and from all accounts an unusually clever woman. She was in a large measure responsible for her husband's popularity in New Orleans and also in Mexico when he was stationed there as viceroy.

Joseph Milhet and Margarethe Catherine Wiltz had two daughters; one was Margarethe Catherine. She was a small child when her father was killed. But in 1782 she had become an attractive young lady. Rousseau had met her several times at the homes of the socialites,, and she had been somewhat impressed with him. He had a good voice and could sing in French, Spanish, and English. When he made a map of the territory in preparation for the capture of Pensacola he disguised himself as a fisherman and went about singing gaily along the banks of the channel which the English held. He sang English and French songs, and the British soldiers gathered around him — and told him all he wished to know. Thus he was a favorite among the social set, and Margarethe Catherine enjoyed his company. But to her he was a rugged soldier "who took his fun where he found it," and she did not take him seriously. She was to him a dainty and pretty girl he wished to marry, and since he was a man of great determination she was not likely to escape him.

He danced with her one evening at the home of

---

* Antoine Maxent, a Spanish officer in New Orleans, was a partner of *Pierre Laclede Liguest,* who was born in Bion, France, near the base of the Pyrenees mountains, in 1724. Very handsome and highly intelligent, he amassed a great fortune, and was one of the founders of St. Louis. He set out to visit New Orleans, and died of a fever when he was about half way on the journey, June 20, 1778. He was never married. If he had relatives entitled to his property, they were unknown. Neither were they sought. Maxent got possession of his property and disposed of it for a trifling sum, and left no slab to his memory.

Don Andres Almonester and during an intermission they walked leisurely along to the end of the long gallery. The moon was full and bright. "I am in love with you," he said.

"In love!" she exclaimed in surprise. "I-ve only met you twice."

"I was in love the first time," he said.

She was frightened. "I think we'd better go inside," she said. "You should sing a French song, please."

"No," said Pierre George, "we must stay here until I have your answer."

"Answer? Answer to what." she asked.

"Surely you know what I mean."

"Not the slightest idea," she said. "But if it's marriage, the answer is no."

"Then," said he, "we shall go inside, and perhaps I shall ask your mother."

She stamped the floor. "You will not. Or I will tell you this: if she says yes I will say no, I think. But I'm not sure. You are an American officer and a great hero. But you're too old; I'm too young, and I have a temper."

"I'm not an old man," thundered Rousseau. "I'm only thirty-one." "But," he said softly, "I may be old in experience."

"I know," said Catherine; "you're the talk of the town. Some say you are a rough American; some say you're a cultured Frenchman; and some say you are related to the great Spanish nobles of the Bourbon tribe, and that is why you were so eager to join Galvez."

"That is not true," said Pierre George. "The Continental navy ordered me to assist Galvez, and when the American Revolution was over he requested me to remain in the Spanish service."

"How strange," she said, "to be of so many nationalities at the same time: you were born a Frenchman, you became an American, and now you are a Spaniard, Don Pedro Rousseau; that is' what they call you."

As this couple saw Almonester approaching they went into the house and Pierre George sang a French song.

There is no record of any other conversation between Pierre George and Margarethe Catherine during their courtship. But there is a clear record of their marriage.

There was not a vacant seat in the old Church of St. Louis when on August 28, 1783 Pierre George Rousseau and Margarethe Catherine Milhet walked up the aisle to be declared man and wife by the Right Reverend Cyrilo Barcelona, Bishop of Louisiana. The witnesses were Margarethe Wiltz Milhet (Panis), Andres Armesto, and Leonardo Mazange.

Don Estevan Miro Becomes Governor of Louisiana When Galvez is Made Viceroy of Mexico

Pierre George Rousseau remained in New Orleans a long time after his marriage. There was quietness on every front, for the people (including the Indians) were tired of war. Galvez, having been awarded the Cross of the Royal Order of Charles III, the title of Count, Lieutenant General of the Army, and Captain General of Florida and Louisiana, sailed early in 1785 for Havana, leaving the government of Louisiana in charge of Estevan Miro, while he himself retained full authority, and gave instructions by letter. But when he was appointed viceroy of Mexico, succeeding his father, who had recently died, Miro became governor of Louisiana. He had been acting as "Juez de Residencia" (Judge of the Residence), and ordered by the Spanish government to inquire into the acts of Governor Unzaga. At this time and during his term as governor (1785-91) he was a virtual tyrant. Severe and narrow, he did not hesitate to interfere in the most private concerns, quite as the Puritan leaders did in early New England. He even wished to regulate the dress of the people, especially of the women. When he became governor he promptly closed the stores, saloons, and shops on Sundays and holidays. He warned the women of the town not to pay "excessive attention to dress," and the mulattoes of the community were definitely forbidden to wear jewelry and plumes. They were required to wear turbans. Work of any kind on Sunday was strictly prohibited. No meeting could be held without a permit from him. Persons entering the city were required to present themselves at the government house to procure a permit to remain for a specified period; and upon leaving were required to give security for the payment of their debts if any had been incurred.

Although there was no actual war in progress at this time, there was trouble regarding the navigation of the Mississippi. The Spanish governors claimed that free navigation was not stipulated in the treaty of peace between England and the United States. The Americans made free use of the River anyway. Miro could not stop them. There was also trouble with the merchants of the colony who had advanced money to Oliver Pollock for the American Revolution. Many suits were filed. In those times a man would sue "at the drop of a hat!"

Trouble with The Pollocks

Oliver Pollock, who had been Commercial Agent at New Orleans for the Continental Congress during the American Revolution, and most helpful to Galvez, refused to submit to these regulations imposed upon the people. Mrs. Pollock especially was very displeased. Nobody was going to tell her how to dress. When she and her husband received an invitation to a ball given by the GENTLEMEN OF THE COUNCIL, she wrote the following letter of refusal:

> I return the Honorable Gentlemen of the Council thanks for the polite Invitation and am Extremely Sorry that I cannot do myself the honor of going to this Ball.
>
> I have the Honor to be gentlemen Your most obe't servant
> Marg't Pollock
>
> Jan. 26, 1783

The Spanish authorities several months later arrested Mrs. Pollock's Negro cook "for a crime" but did not say what crime. This infuriated her, and she wrote to Miro.

> Sir; please to lay peek a oneside let reason & Justice take place and return me my Cook that I Certainle do Mise and certain it is that you have no Right to detain her upon any protence whatever
>
> I am your Excell'y. Most obedient Sirvant.
> Marg't Pollock
>
> 1783

This letter angered Miro, and he wrote to Mrs. Pollock:

My Dear Madam: Your letter is very insulting to the authority of the government, as well as the expressions you saw fit to make use of a few days ago. If you continue, I shall let you know that the government has authority over women. Your negress is accused of a crime which must be tried according to the laws. These will condemn her, if guilty, or absolve her, if proved innocent. I advise you that I shall accept no other letter from you, and if you have anything to communicate to me, you may do so by means of a petition.

May God preserve your life many years.
New Orleans, September 13, 1783
Madam Margaret Pollock

(Draft by Miro)

Mrs. Pollock ignored Miro's request to communicate with him only by means of a petition and sent him a bitter reply on the same day. She wrote:

SIR: So you threaten me. I think you, Sir, as to your Credentials agaenst Ladies very possible but my own opinion is natural & obvious that the greateste Difficulty does not Lay in making one feel their influence for the moment, Sir I doubt not but you will order my Servant out of Confinement not that I so much feel the Loss of hir, but humanity obliges me to speak in the behalf of the feeble & the Innocent, it is well known that she has been ill treated by those People that dreads not the Laws of God or man. I am told that sometime ago, that there have been a band Published for their Refermation Sir as to Present you with a Petition be assured were I to attempt it, it would only inflame me to the highest degree, & would of Course perish in the Exertion, it makes no difference what Part of the King of Spains Dominions that Mr. Pollock resedes in, he is equally Indebted to render him Justice. I hope you will not answer this letter — . . . .
New Orleans 13th Sept'r. 1783
Yo'r Mo't.Obe't

Marg't Pollock

His Excellency Stephen Miro

Although the AGI papers do not say what happened to Mrs. Pollock's cook, there is evidence that the controversy did not end with the letter which she requested

Miro not to answer. For in a letter to Miro dated October 24, 1783, Oliver Pollock says: "I confess I feel myself too much hurt to dwell longer on this subject, so shall solely add, that in the case of the Person I hold most dear, does not merit the former friendship and politeness your Excell'y once pleased to honour us with, I hope your Excell'y will not forget what is due her Sex. very obed't & humble Serv't. Ol'r Pollock."

Oliver Pollock had advanced the United States $300,-000.00 during the early part of the Revolution out of his own pocket, and there is no record to show that this money was ever returned to him. Then Galvez had advanced Oliver Pollock $20,000 to buy arms and ammunition for the American Revolution. But Spain had declared war on England on May 8, 1779, and on July 8, 1779 the American subjects of Charles III were authorized to take part in the war. Henceforth Spain and the United States were in the war together. The continental Congress had already considered the advisability of an attack on Pensacola and Mobile at a meeting of a Board of War as early as July 10, 1777. The members present were: Mr. John Adams, Mr. Harrison, Mr. Wilson, Mr. George Clymer, Mr. S. Adams, and Mr. Duer. It was proposed: "That an Expedition be undertaken against Pensacola and Mobile in West Florida to facilitate which, that Colonel George Morgan be sent to New Orleans with Power to negotiate with the governor of that Place; and endeavor to gain his interest and assistance in the business; and that One thousand Men will be necessary for this Service, and the Command of the Expedition be given to General Hand. . . . ."

This plan of attack was not, of course, carried out until 1781 by Galvez himself after he had made ample preparation. Meantime Oliver Pollock, as commercial agent for the Continental Congress, was called upon to supply ammunitions and other necessities for the American forces stationed in the vicinity of New Orleans. Thus he was compelled to borrow money and buy materials on credit, for the resources of the United States government were at the time very limited. After the war the Spanish colonial government and the private citizens from whom he had borrowed money or procured goods on credit were pressing him for payment. He advised them repeatedly that these loans and bills could only be paid by the treasury of the United States, and that he had submitted them for payment. He had urged his government to act promptly in the matter.

Still they pressed him, not always politely. They had forgotten his generosity to the people during the administration of O'Reilly, when they were in dire need. They knew that he was eminently successful as a merchant and also eminently trustworthy as a man. But they imposed upon these qualities conditions beyond his ability to sustain his reputation.

> "Blow, blow, thou winter wind!
> Thou art not so unkind
> As man's ingratitude."

Obviously the tyranny of the Spanish officers and the ingratitude of their government irked Mrs. Pollock, who was a woman of considerable courage, and that was actually her reason for returning the invitation to the "Ball of the Gentlemen of the Council," which was to be a gala affair attended only by members of the exclusive social set.

John Walton Caughey in "Bernardo de Galvez in Louisiana" says that it would be "difficult to overestimate Pollock's contributions to the success of the Revolution . . . . Liberal though Galvez was in advancing government funds, American needs could have not been met if Pollock had not made use of his personal fortune and credit. He did so without stint so long as he possessed either, and he succeeded in paying Clark's drafts at par in New Orleans when Continental currency was worth only twelve cents on the dollar in the East." He sometimes had to borrow at 12½ per cent to meet drafts, and when eventually the merchants of New Orleans refused to lend him money for the Revolution (only because they were doubtful that it would ever be paid) he was compelled to mortgage his own property to get it. He had raised in one instance the sum of $136,000 for the American cause, and although this was an obligation of the state of Virginia, and recognized as such by the House of Delegates, it was obvious that the loans were procured because of his good standing, and that he was considered responsible for their payment. Virginia and the United States did not remit this amount until many years later. Meantime Pollock was arrested in Havana for debts due the New Orleans merchants. Galvez procured his release, and he was permitted to go to Philadelphia to make arrangements to satisfy his creditors. Galvez advanced him the money for this purpose. Although this money was from the public treasury, it was eventually paid to Galvez' estate.

Louis Houck says in his SPANISH REGIME IN MISSOURI that Oliver Pollock came to New Orleans in 1769, General O'Reilly then being in command of the country.. He arrived in the Brig Royal Charlotte, loaded with flour, and at the time, owing to scarcity of flour, it sold for 30 dollars a barrel. Finding this to be the situation, he waited on General O'Reilly and offered his cargo of flour and told him to fix the price on it; this O'Reilly declined. Pollock then said that as the King had three thousand troops there, and needed flour, he did not wish to take advantage of the situation and offered his flour at 15 dollars a barrel, to which O'Reilly readily agreed, and observed that he would make a note of his liberality and that as long as he was in command he should have free trade there. This trade he enjoyed, and when O'Reilly left he recommended him to Unzaga, and Unzaga to Galvez, etc. When the Revolution began Pollock was appointed representative of the United Colonies at New Orleans, enjoying the confidence of the Spanish officials. At various times he received from them secret service money, amounting to 75,000 dollars to be disbursed for the benefit of the colonies.

Pollock actually received this seventy-five thousand dollars from Galvez after Spain declared war on England (1779) to be forwarded to the colonies for the purpose of purchasing arms and ammunition.

Oliver Pollock was the first American merchant to establish himself in New Orleans.

Rousseau Appointed Commandant at Natchitoches

Natchitoches, which is the oldest city in Louisiana, was an important military and trading post under both the French and Spanish regimes. It was founded in 1714 by the French. Situated near the Red River, it is one of the most picturesque spots in Louisiana. To be stationed as commandant there was a very agreeable appointment.

On March 5, 1785, Galvez gave Rousseau permission to go to France, and advised Miro that the GALVEZ-TOWN, which had been constantly under Rousseau's command, should be sent to Havana under another command if it was not presently on duty. His visit to France was concerning a personal matter, for his family owned an estate at Arles and held some property also at La Tremblade.

While he was on his way to France, Galvez appointed him commandant at Natchitoches, and when he returned he assumed command at this post, which he held until March 1, 1787, when he delivered the command to Louis de Blanc, and went to New Orleans on leave of absence. He returned to the post, however, at the end of 1788 and again assumed command. He had an interest also in the command of the post at Natchez, where Gayoso de Lemos was stationed as "governor of the post," and divided his time between the two places.

The following is the letter from Galvez, dated April 6, 1785, advising Miro that he had appointed Rousseau commandant at Natchitoches:

> To serve as political and military commandant of the post of Natchitoches, at present in charge of the Infantry Captain Don Pedro Estevan Vaugine, I have appointed Army Captain Don Pedro Rousseau, in view of the distinguished services which he has rendered; and I advise Your Lordship of this so that you on your part may issue the orders you may think advisable for the proper compliance with this action.

May God preserve Your Lordship many years.
Havana, 6th of April, 1785

El Conde de Galvez (Rubric)

Senor Don Estevan Miro

The Appointment

DON ESTEVAN MIRO, etc: Since there is a vacancy in the command at the post of Natchitoches, due to the retirement of Captain Don Estevan Vaugine who held it, and since it is advisable to appoint as his successor a person of good conduct, zeal, and experience, by order of said Senor as expressed in official communication of the 6th of April of the present year, we have appointed and by these presents do hereby appoint Don Pedro Rousseau, infantry captain, to serve in said post, inasmuch as he combines all the stated personal qualifications.

Therefore, we order military officers, sergeants, corporals of night guards, and other residents of said post of Natchitoches to regard and consider him as such commandant and obey all orders, verbal or in writing, which he might give on behalf of the royal service for policing, good government, and administration of justice of said post. To this end we issue these presents signed by our hand and sealed with the seal of our arms and authenticated by the undersigned secretary of this government in New Orleans, the 4th of July, 1785.

His Lordship appoints as commandant of the post of Natchitoches, Captain of the Army Don Pedro Rousseau.

(Attached to the foregoing)

Instructions which must be observed by Army Captain Don Pedro Rousseau, appointed by the most Excellent Condé de Galvez, viceroy of New Spain and Captain general of these provinces, as commandant, for the post of Natchitoches.

---

95 AGI, PC, leg. 11.

1st. Your first and principal concern upon arrival at the post will be to win the esteem of those residents, and establish by all practicable means, union and harmony, making your rule pleasant by forbearance without at the same time being lax in administering justice and without digressing one point from the orders he might receive from the supreme government.

2nd. Likewise you shall cultivate the most perfect co-operation with the governor of the province of Texas and commandant of the presidio of Nuestra Senora del Pilar de Nacogdoches, co-operating with said chiefs to hold the nations of Indians located between the Interior Provinces and this of Louisiana tranquil and peaceful, which object is particularly recommended by the court.

3rd. No trader is to have access to the nations without special permission from me, and in case any of them in the district should be without a trader, you shall propose one to me. For your part, do all you can to see that the nations of the district under your command be provided with traders of good manners and habits; and you shall take special care that they do not incur larger debts than they can pay, which can easily be avoided by seeing that they meet their obligations punctually by being on the watch that they enter the post every year, and not permitting them to accumulate supplies from various persons.

4th. You shall absolutely prohibit any foreigner from having commercial dealings with the Indians. If, notwithstanding, any one should accomplish this, you shall endeavor to arrest him and send him to the capital at a convenient opportunity.

5th. On no pretext are you to allow settlement of Americans in this district, and you shall report to me if there is any.

6th. You shall not permit anyone to establish himself there without express orders from me to that effect; and neither shall those already established, although being free to move to another district as their convenience or interests demand, be permitted to do so without the express consent of the supreme government.

7th. You shall actively promote the cultivation of tobacco, in view of the particular advantage redounding to the residents, as well as to the general benefits to the province.

8th. Every year you shall draw up a general census of your district, as has been the custom of your predecessors.

9th. You are to maintain closest co-operation with the Reverend Parish Priest, whose high personal qualifications merit every confidence. Furthermore, it is much easier to control the behavior and manage the subjects when the chiefs work in harmony.

10th. The special provisions of these instructions do not annul those made for the command of Natchitoches on various occasions by the most Excellent Condé de O'Reilly, Field Marshall Don Luis de Unzaga y Amezaga, and the most excellent captain general of these provinces, which you will find in the archives of that post. To these you shall strictly adhere, unless, due to circumstances at the time, you should have orders to the contrary from the supreme government.

11th. The abuse of the escrituras and special contracts called sous seing prive is very injurious and must be rigidly curtailed to avoid the continuous strife and complications that occupy the attention of the government, and distract the inhabitants from their work, for which reason you shall not allow any of those escrituras to be executed in any other way than before Your Lordship and the two assistant witnesses.

12th. By no means is your Lordship to allow any trader or resident to make a slave of or purchase any Indian. Advise me by first opportunity if there are any at the post, who their masters are, how they acquired them, and the time they have had them. If there is found to be any abuse, it is indispensable that it be cut off at the root.

13th. In the incursions made by the Indians from the north on the presidios and frontiers of the Kingdom of New Spain there were many Spanish families who were captured and who even now suffer under the cruel yoke of barbarism, with great risks to their salvation. Your Lordship shall never lose any opportunity which is presented to rescue as many as possible, sending me a report of the results obtained, and making a special request on my behalf in this regard to the trader Armand and others engaged in those nations.

14th. You will direct the administration of justice according to the dictates of our learned laws, to which end you will be presented by the secretary of this government the Book of Instructions arranged by order of Condé de O'Reilly.

Lastly, I trust that in your activity, prudence, and zeal for the service, those inhabitants will consider themselves fortunate to be under your authority and that the superior government will not experience the past anxieties and vexations. I leave to your judgement whatever may not be found covered in the above mentioned instructions and in the present document.

NEW ORLEANS, 4th of July, 1785.

A letter from Miro to Cruzat, dated March 24, 1786, throws some light upon what was happening at Natchitoches. Miro says:

Rousseau was commandant at Natchitoches March 24, 1786, for in a letter from Miro to Cruzat (of that date) Miro says: " . . . the commandant of Natchitoches, Don Pedro Rousseau, advises me, and his information finds confirmation in Arkansas, that there has been a sharp encounter between the Caddo Indians and a band of the Little Osage from the settlement on the Arkansas River. The former, returning from the hunt with their horses and many furs, were attacked by a numerous party of the second nation. The combat became violent and lasted, so they say, from morning until late at night when it came to an end because the Caddos found themselves without any ammunition and with two dead and two wounded. As a result they took advantage of the darkness in order to make their escape. The Kichaï have been equally pillaged by the aforesaid Osage and have lost four men, their horses, and the product of their hunt, not being able to kill more than one of the enemy."

Letter begins pg. 171 — Vol. 3 — 11

Spain in the Mississippi Valley

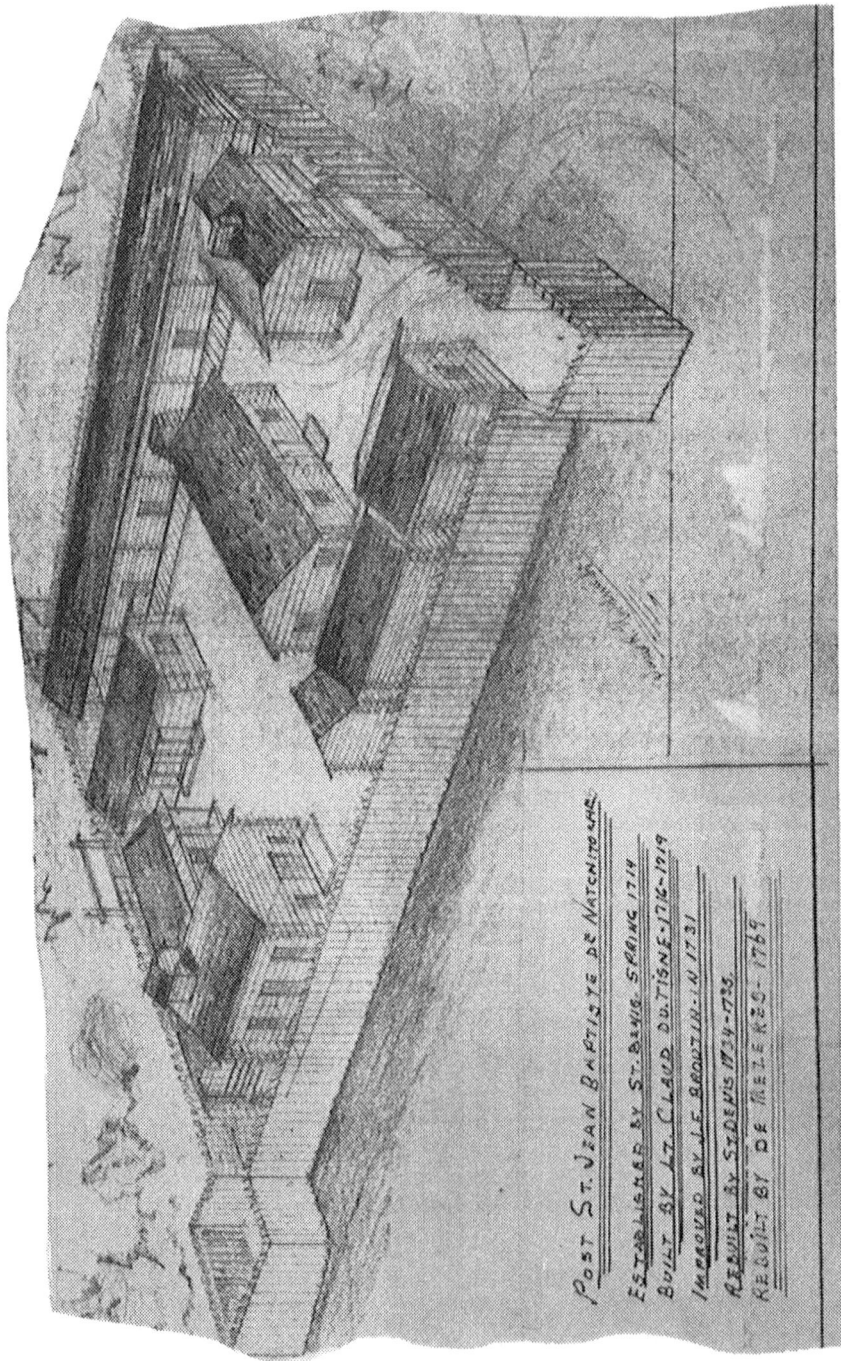

POST ST. JEAN BAPTISTE DE NATCHITOCHES

ESTABLISHED BY ST. DAVIS SPRING 1714
BUILT BY LT. CLAUD DU. TISNE - 1716 - 1219
IMPROVED BY LE. BROUTIN - IN 1731
REBUILT BY ST DENIS 1734 - 1735.
REBUILT BY DE MEZERES - 1765

The fort at Natchitoches where Rousseau resided while Commandant there

Miro Leaves Louisiana[1]

Although Estevan Miro had married a native of New Orleans (Celeste Elenore Elizabeth de Macarty) he was not satisfied to make his home permanently in Louisiana but always looked forward to the time when he could return to Spain. His administration had not been without trying problems. Among the difficulties and annoyances with which he was confronted were: (1) The arrival of Father Antonio de Sedella, who was sent by his spiritual superiors to Louisiana as a representative of the Inquisition, with the purpose of establishing a branch of that tribunal in New Orleans. But he had him arrested and promptly sent back to Spain. (Father Sedella eventually returned to New Orleans and became a favorite of the people; not, however, as an agent of the Inquisition but as an ordinary priest who taught Christianity and nothing more.) (2) The fire of 1788, which destroyed 856 houses, the St. Louis Cathedral, the convent of the Capuchins, the Town Hall, and the arsenal, making it necessary virtually to rebuild the city. (3) The Western people's threat to invade Louisiana and seize New Orleans, causing considerable unrest, and compelling him to stand constantly on guard. He had handled these matters with wisdom and efficiency. In 1791 he was permitted to retire from Louisiana and return to Spain with his family.

He was succeeded by Carondelet, whose administration, though fraught with difficulties, marked the beginning of improvements and progress which changed New Orleans from a mere village into a thriving city.

---

[1] Miro remained as governor of Louisiana longer than any other Spaniard.

FRANCOIS LOUIS HECTOR, Baron de Carondelet

Carondelet Appointed Governor of Louisiana

Francois Louis Hector, Baron de Carondelet de Noyelles, Seigneur d'Haine St. Pierre, was born in 1747 in Flanders. He was of an illustrious family, which originated with Jean de Charond, chancellor of Bourgoyne, so that his family was of Bourguignonne origin, and became Flemish at the end of the fifteenth century. The name arose from the founder, Charond, who was called Carondelet because of his small figure, and which indeed seems to have been a family characteristic, because Carondelet also was of short stature. Although there is no direct authority, it is supposed that he entered the Spanish military service in the Walloon Guards, and thus came into the Spanish colonial service. Before he was appointed Governor of Louisiana he was Governor of San Salvador in Guatemala. He arrived at

New Orleans in January of 1792 to succeed Miro as governor of the colony.

From the very beginning he was active in promoting every enterprise calculated to advance the prosperity of the colony. He greatly improved the municipal administration of New Orleans; he introduced a system for lighting the streets, fortified the city, built the canal known as the Carondelet Canal, which drained the city and gave it water connection with Lake Pontchartrain, and during his administration the first newspaper was published in New Orleans. In 1797 he was appointed President of THE ROYAL AUDIENCIA OF QUITA, ECUADOR.

Carondelet Fears an "Invasion" of Louisiana, and Instructs Gayoso, Commandant at Natchez, To Order Rousseau to Make a Thorough Investigation

The redoubtable William Augustus Bowles and others of his ilk had advised Carondelet that General James Wilkinson and General George R. Clark, in cooperation with the French minister to the United States, Edmond C. Genet, were attempting to organize an expedition in the west against Spanish possessions. Auguste de la Chaise of Louisiana was also implicated in this scheme; he acted as Genet's agent in Kentucky. It was rumored that thousands of troops were being raised in Georgia and the Carolinas to invade the provinces of Spain, and Carondelet wrote to Luis de las Casas, the governor at Cuba, assuring him that Rousseau "would arrive New Madrid with his squadron of galleys ready to attack the enemy as they leave the Ohio," if he found it necessary. But he wished to ascertain how serious the situation was, and that is why he instructed Gayoso to order Rousseau to make the investigation; that is, to "embark on the secret expedition," which resulted in the writing of the (following) log, which is an interesting account of the "situation as it was."

As a matter of fact, the whole scheme had been upset by Washington, who bitterly opposed it when brought to his attention. The Americans who enlisted in Genet's privateers at Charleston were put to trial, and Genet's recall was requested.

Genet was supported in his scheme by the French Jacobins of Philadelphia, who, as the Jacobins of France, advocated war to discredit the monarchy.

Captain Pierre George Rousseau's
LOG OF
HIS MAJESTY'S GALIOT, La Fleche,
January 5 to March 25, 1793

SATURDAY, JANUARY 5, 1793.

At two o'clock in the afternoon I received the order from Don Manuel Gayoso de Lemos, governor of the post of Natchez, to embark on a secret expedition on the galiot of war, La Fleche, armed with eight bronze swivel guns, and with a crew of eighteen men, and three soldiers of the regiment of Louisiana. I intrusted the command of my squadron to Mr. Gayoso who took charge of it. At 3 o'clock in the morning I received a sealed packet which Mr. Gayoso de Lemos, governor of Natchez, delivered to me with the order to sail. At four o'clock, I set sail and passed the night one league from Natchez.*

SUNDAY, JANUARY 6, 1793.

Set sail at 6 o'clock in the morning. At five o'clock in the evening encamped 5 leagues from Natchez. There came alongside a canoe from the galleys which brought me two sacks of biscuit and a letter from the governor of Natchez.

MONDAY, JANUARY 7, 1793.

At 6 o'clock in the morning set sail, the weather very cold; at 5 o'clock at night encamped 10 leagues from Natchez.

---

* Lawrence Kinnaird, "Spain in the Mississippi Valley"

TUESDAY, JANUARY 8, 1793.

At 6 o'clock in the morning set sail, against high head winds; at 5 o'clock at night encamped one league below the Bayou aux Pierres. Traveled six leagues.

WEDNESDAY, JANUARY 9, 1793.

At 6 o'clock in the morning set sail against a head wind. At 8 o'clock across from the Bayou aux Pierres a barge and a pirogue came alongside. They came from Illinois, and their proprietor was named Cerré. He told me nothing new, that all was very peaceful up above, that he was going to New Orleans loaded with furs. At the same hour there came alongside two pirogues which had just come from Arkansas loaded with furs and salt belonging to Mr. Menard, who was aboard and who was going to New Orleans. At 5 o'clock encamped half a league above the Grand Gulf.

THURSDAY, JANUARY 10, 1793.

At 6 o'clock in the morning started out, rowing. The wind ahead had almost died down. At 5 o'clock at night encamped below three islands. Made five leagues and a half. The weather was very cold and foggy.

FRIDAY, JANUARY 11, 1793.

At 6 o'clock in the morning set out, the weather calm. At 9 o'clock in the morning a stump under the water hit our rudder and broke the iron-work. At five o'clock encamped at the base of Nogales Island. Made six leagues and a half in three hours.

SATURDAY, JANUARY 12, 1793.

Started at 6 o'clock in the morning with a little favorable wind. At 3 o'clock in the afternoon the commandant of Nogales, Don Elie Beauregard, and the guard of the magazine of said post came alongside in a canoe. At 4 o'clock stopped before the Fort of Nogales. I immediately sent an official letter to the commandant to have him make for me an iron binding for the rudder and have him give me 100 cartridges of musket shot and 6 pounds of ball and a packet of cord, which we had forgotten on embarking from Natchez, and two ox hides to put over the load because the water ran through the tarpaulins. All of these things I received from him.

MONDAY, JANUARY 14, 1793.

At 10 o'clock in the morning the iron binding for my rudder was ready and put in place to set sail. As I was going to leave, a barge arrived. I went on board to visit it and to find out whence it came. They told me that they had just come from Fort Pitt, that its owners were on board, that their names were William Moore and Robert Scott. It appeared to me to be laden with merchandise. The weather so bad that I was not able to start.

TUESDAY, JANUARY 15, 1793.

The wind so strong from the direction of the north that I could not set sail. I observed the latitude of the Fort of Nogales as 32 degrees 14 minutes north. At ten o'clock at night I observed the longitude of said place as 95 degrees 20 minutes from the London meridian.

WEDNESDAY, JANUARY 16, 1793.

The wind having calmed, I traveled from 7 o'clock in the morning until 5 o'clock at night when I encamped one half league from the River of the Yazoos. The weather is fair; made four leagues.

THURSDAY, JANUARY 17, 1793.

Set sail at 6 o'clock in the morning, the weather calm. At 10 o'clock in the morning passed a large island on the west side; passed between the land and said island; at 3 o'clock in the afternoon passed a small and a large island near the same bank. Encamped at 5 o'clock; traveled five and a half leagues. The weather fair, probability of rain.

FRIDAY, JANUARY 18, 1793.

At 6 o'clock in the morning set sail, the wind favorable; at half past 10 in the morning passed four islands on the east side. Scarcely any water flowed between the land and the said islands. The shallows extended to great width and went nearly to the middle of the river which greatly lengthened our course.

SATURDAY, JANUARY 19, 1793.

At six o'clock in the morning started off, the weather calm. At 8 o'clock passed several islands near the west bank, made the great turn; at 4 o'clock in the afternoon passed three islands; at 5 o'clock encamped above the three islands.

SUNDAY, JANUARY 20, 1793.

Set out at 6 o'clock in the morning, the wind favorable, set the sail. At 1 o'clock passed a little island in the middle of the river; at 5 o'clock at night encamped on the island called Death's Head. Made 8 leagues, the weather fair, but very cold.

MONDAY, JANUARY 21, 1793.

At 6 o'clock in the morning set sail, the wind ahead. At 9 o'clock the wind was so strong that it obliged me to encamp until the morrow on an island near the west bank at one league from Death's Head. The weather was very cold and the current very swift.

TUESDAY, JANUARY 22, 1793.

At 6 o'clock in the morning began to travel, sailing, the wind good and fresh. At 5 o'clock in the evening encamped at the foot of the island of La Coupeé on the west side. The island is near the same shore. Went nine and a half leagues on this day's journey. The weather is fair, the currents very strong.

WEDNESDAY, JANUARY 23, 1793.

Set out at 6 o'clock in the morning; at noon put to shore for dinner. While we were on shore, there came from above by the west bank twenty-five Choctaws with their wives and children and fifteen horses laden with pelts; and two pirogues loaded with skins, manned by two Indian men and four women, came down by the river. There was among them a half-breed who spoke very good English. He told me that he had just been hunting on the west bank of the Mississippi and that he was returning to his village which was the one in which Mr. Delavillebeuvre resides, and that he had crossed the river yesterday in the morning. I asked him if he had seen anyone since he left his village. He replied that he had not seen any white men, that ten days ago he had met a party of fifteen Chickasaws with their women who were leaving their village, but that he had said nothing to them. He asked me to trade for their pelts. I replied that my boat was a royal vessel and that I traded with no one. He asked me for some tafia. I told him I did not have any. He asked me for a little bread and I gave them 24 sea biscuit and afterwards set sail and left them encamped at the same place. At 5 o'clock in the evening I encamped on the west bank, having passed twice by the east. Made five leagues and a half.

THURSDAY, JANUARY 24, 1793.

At 6 o'clock in the morning set out, the wind ahead. Found a swift current and very extensive shallows. At noon put to shore to prepare dinner; at half past one saw 2 barges which were drifting. I motioned to them to come ashore. They came from the Belle Riviere to hunt. One was rowed by some Frenchmen who had a passport from Mr. Zenon Trudeau, commandant of St. Louis in Illinois. I gave them a letter for the governor of Natchez. The other was manned by some Americans from Kentucky who had left there three months ago and who were hunting on the Belle Riviere. They told me that the Cherokees and the Creeks attacked the post of Cumberland before their departure, killed several persons, and burned several houses and withdrew, and that near Fort Washington they had attacked an American party, killing several soldiers, carrying off 60 horses and fleeing with what they had taken. Purchased 60 pounds of salted meat. Sailed; at 5 o'clock in the evening encamped. Made 6 leagues according to my reckoning.

FRIDAY, JANUARY 25, 1793.

Began to travel at 6 o'clock in the morning. The wind being favorable, we put up the sail. At 10 o'clock we passed an island near the east bank; at noon saw a savage on the west bank, recognized him as an Arkansas; at 4 o'clock in the afternoon passed the Isle aux Chicots; hailed a barge which was manned by some

Americans and which came from the Wabash loaded with salted meat; at the same hour saw a barge, which we did not recognize, pass on the other side of the island; at 5 o'clock in the evening encamped. Traveled six leagues.

SATURDAY, JANUARY 26, 1793.

At 6 o'clock in the morning set out with the sails and the oars. At 9 o'clock saw a barge which was going down the river. I made it come alongside. It came from the Arkansas and its master was named Bougigue. On board were 4 men and equipment and Mr. Vaugine Jr. with a passport from Mr. Delino, commandant of Arkansas. It was going to New Orleans laden with skins and salted meat. I gave him a letter for the governor of Natchez and I set sail. During the same hour I passed a superb cypress grove, one league below the three channels, 12 leagues from the Arkansas River. At noon passed the three channels. All the morning we had a little rain. At 5 o'clock in the evening camped on a point on the east side. At 7 o'clock an Arkansas savage came to our encampment with two women. He told us that he was encamped on the other bank of the river, that he was hunting, and that we were 6 points from the Arkansas River. Traveled six and a half leagues according to my reckoning.

SUNDAY, JANUARY 27, 1793.

At 6 o'clock resumed our journey, the wind good, set the sail. Passed between two islands near the west bank; at noon passed among six islands, found a strong current, did not land for dinner, but proceeded, the wind being favorable; at 3 o'clock passed an island on the east side; at 6 o'clock encamped across from the large Isle au Bled on the west side, at 2 leagues from the Arkansas River. There is the appearance of bad weather. Made seven leagues and a half.

MONDAY, JANUARY 28, 1793.

Started at 6 o'clock in the morning in a high wind, a very strong head wind. At noon we had gone only one league. We were below the little Isle au Bled. As it appeared to us that there was some water, we wished to pass on the inside, but when we went to the outlet, we found scarcely any water. We were obliged to return to the foot of the island. The wind blew continuously from the north, strong and fresh. While we were at the upper end of the island, there passed two drifting barges and a pirogue which turned off and were out of sight when we reached the lower end of the island. At 5 o'clock in the evening encamped on the east shore at one league from the mouth of the Arkansas River. The wind was very strong from the north; the weather overcast and very cold with the probability of snow.

TUESDAY, JANUARY 29, 1793.

At 6 o'clock sailed, with the wind very high from the northeast, to reach the Arkansas River. At 9 o'clock entered the said river. My coxswain having pointed out that it was impossible to continue our voyage with the iron bindings of our rudder broken. For four days we had been holding them with cords. I therefore determined to stop at the Arkansas post to put my rudder in condition to continue my voyage. At noon the weather was so bad and the wind so high, with snow falling, that I was obliged to encamp half a league from the Arkansas River. All day the wind and the snow lasted. We were glad to be sheltered from the bad weather and the wind.

WEDNESDAY, JANUARY 30, 1793.

Remained in camp all day, the weather terrible, the snow continuously falling, there being two feet of snow on the ground. Northeast wind, very cold. At 4 o'clock the wind shifted northwards, very strong, everything frozen.

THURSDAY, JANUARY 31, 1793.

The weather remains very cold, the wind very strong from the northwest until noon when it calmed. I set out at once. Made 3 points on the river and at 5 o'clock encamped.

FRIDAY, FEBRUARY 1, 1793.

Resumed the journey at 6 o'clock in the morning, the weather continuing cold. By noon had made 6 points and arrived at the fork of the White River. Followed the Arkansas River; at 5 o'clock encamped. From the entrance of the river to the point there are 11 points. Made six points in the Arkansas River since noon. The river is very bad, full of stumps, and having a swift current and the shoals are very dangerous. The water is as red as in the River Rouge at the post of Natchitoches.

SATURDAY, FEBRUARY 2, 1793.

Began to travel at half past 6, the weather bad. It is raining. Two hours later arrived at the Arkansas post. I went ashore to ask the commandant if he had some blacksmiths. He replied that he had an old Negro. I requested that he send for him immediately in order that he might take the measurements of the iron bindings of my rudder to make new ones and to mend the old ones also. The Negro came and took the measurements. All day it rained and was very cold.

SUNDAY, FEBRUARY 3, 1793.

The wind from the northwest blew a fresh gale and very cold. The Arkansas post is situated on the side óf a hill which overlooks the Arkansas River. It may be 45 feet in height when the river is low, and when it is high, 6 feet. It forms a horseshoe which extends towards the north about half a league. Half a league north of the river there is a great prairie which follows the shoe and extends to Illinois, as one of the inhabitants told me. There are several inhabitants around the prairie who sow the wheat which I have seen. It is very. beautiful.

The Arkansas fort is surrounded on all sides by a stockade of white oaks to shelter it from rifle-fire. It has one bastion on the east and another on the west, in which are mounted a cannon of four and two swivel guns. There are in the fort a house, headquarters, and a storehouse covered with shingles. Outside the fort there are thirty houses, with galleries around them, and covered with shingles. They form two streets below the fort.

There are a dozen quite pretty houses on plots of 4 by 4 arpents. There are some very good looking wheat fields on the high land. Below the high land all the surface is under water. The savages appear very docile and very attached to the Spaniards. There are three villages each ruled by its chief. The sun being favorable, I observed the latitude of the fort with the quadrant and it is 34 degrees and 6 minutes north.

MONDAY, FEBRUARY 4, 1793.

The day broke badly with rain. At noon riveted the iron binding of my rudder, but it was not possible to travel because of the bad weather. I gave the smith who made the new bands for me and mended the old an order for 10 piastres on Don Francisco Arnoyo, ministre interventeur of the town of Natchez. I was obliged to leave two of my sailors at the Arkansas post because of sickness and I gave them orders to meet me at the mouth of the White River, where there was a detachment of three soldiers to pick them up, when they had recovered. Took in their places a Canadian named Semit.

TUESDAY, FEBRUARY 5, 1793.

All day the rain fell. I could not sail. All the oats I had on board were found to be spoiled. I was obliged to buy half a barrel of them. Being at the disadvantage of not having any at the post, they made me pay 3 piastres for a half a barrel near the post.

WEDNESDAY, FEBRUARY 6, 1793.

The weather clearing up a little, I started out at 7 o'clock to descend the Arkansas River. At 10 o'clock rain began to fall so hard that I was obliged to encamp 6 points below the Arkansas. At 3 o'clock the rain ceased to fall. I set sail. At half past 5 I encamped at the fork of the two rivers. From the Arkansas post to the fork there are 13 points. The river is very bad, with many snags and little water when it is low.

THURSDAY, FEBRUARY 7, 1793.

Set sail at half past six in the branch of the White River. Made 3 points. Came down on the White River, turned off 3 points, entered the Mississippi. At the outlet of the White River there was an island where two soldiers and a corporal, detached from the Arkansas post, were stationed. At ten o'clock I was in the river and at noon I encamped on a point one league and a half from the White River to prepare dinner and for my company to dry their clothing which was all wet. As I was going to camp a barge, which was descending, appeared. I had it put to shore. It came from New Madrid, with a passport from the commandant of said place, laden with pelts and salt going to New Orleans. Its master was named Pierre Chausson and he had a crew of three men. By the said barge I sent a letter to the governor of the town of Natchez. They told me that everything was very quiet up above, and that there was no sign of anything when they set out.

FRIDAY, FEBRUARY 8, 1793.

Set out at half past five in the morning, the wind good, put up the sail. Was under sail all day; passed four islands; at half past five encamped. Traveled ten leagues.

SATURDAY, FEBRUARY 9, 1793.

Resumed the journey at half past five, the wind ahead. At 11 there came alongside eleven pirogues filled with Chickasaw and Arkansas savages. They asked me to trade. I told them that the King's ships did not trade, and that they could see by my flag and pennant that I was not a trader. They asked me for some tafia. I told them that I had none. They followed me until noon when I landed to get dinner, asking me for some bread. I gave them three dozen sea biscuit and they were all very content.

This is the speech which a Chickasaw half-breed named Thomas, captain of the party, made to me, using very good English.

"My father, when we were at war this summer with the Osages we passed the Arkansas. The chief of the whites told us that the great chief of New Orleans had closed all the roads and had forbidden the white men to carry goods into their villages. Ah! my father, were the Osages deserving of pity? It is we and these Arkansas whom you see here that are, and not the Osages. We have found them well clad in new blankets of Limbourg and wool and all with new guns. My father, they throw goods away in their villages. (Showing me an

Osage woman that he had with him) you see, my father, this Osage woman. She tells the truth. She says that there arrived this summer at their village ten barges or pirogues from Illinois with many white men in them. She recognized the younger Choutaux, and the clerk, and the Negro of Mr. Labady, who were all there.

"Tell me, my father, whether the whites of Illinois are Spanish or our enemies, and if it is necessary to attack them when they carry the booty to Illinois, since you see they carry to our enemies wherewith to kill us. You see that they take guns, powder, and ball to the Osages and buy from them all this booty which they steal from the Spaniards and red men on the rivers and that they kill all the whites of Natchitoches and Arkansas and all the red men of this region who cannot hunt without being killed or plundered by the Osages. You see the Arkansas who cannot go hunting in the prairies without being murdered by the Osages. They are obliged like us to come to hunt deer on the Mississippi while the Osages make themselves masters of all the hunting country.

"The Osages, my father, are at war with all men, white and red. They steal the horses and kill all the white men they find. The white men of Illinois carry goods to them. Ah! my father, if the Osages only had their arrows and they were not given any goods, we would soon finish them. As for peace, we cannot hope for it with them. They have always deceived those with whom they have made it and will never have lasting peace. They have never given a good word to other men. Ah! my father, if the great chief of New Orleans had all those who carry goods to the Osages killed, there would be no one to carry it and a year later we could plan to attack their village when the corn is in milk, for at that time all the Osages are hunting. We could destroy all their corn and make their women and children prisoners as well as their old men. We could place ourselves on the roads by which they would return to their village and we could destroy them all, and those who escaped would die from hunger or would be killed by some other red men."

He sat down on the sand, made a circle and afterwards continued his speech: "My father, you see this circle which I have just made there? The Osages are in the center of it and are surrounded by white and red men and we let them kill us and steal our horses and we leave them alone. If a red man of any other nation kills another, we demand his head and, if he steals a horse, he is punished by his chief. I pray you, my father, carry these words to your great chief so that he may stop the white men of Illinois from carrying goods to the Osages to kill us with. When we went to attack them, they killed two men whom we mourn still. You see, my father, it is we who are deserving of pity and not the Osages as the chief of the Arkansas had told us. You see all these women and children who are here. It is so that they will not die of hunger in the village, for we have raised scarcely any corn this year. We have lost nearly all our horses, which hinders us from going very far to hunt. We are forced to hunt deer on the Mississippi."

After he had ended his speech he asked me for a little gunpowder. I gave him six gun cartridges which I had on hand. As my company had finished dinner, I set out. They remained on land. On putting off they saluted me with seven musket shots. I replied to them with seven shots from the swivel guns. At half past five encamped on the point of an island on the east side. Made five leagues. One hour after we had camped the sentinel cried that some savages were coming. We prepared to receive them if they had evil intentions, but we saw that there were only eight and without arms. On arriving they gave me their hands. We recognized them as Chickasaws. One who spoke a little English told me that they were encamped on the other end of the island, that they saw our fire and came to see what it was. They asked for something to eat. I gave them six sea biscuit. They remained with us nearly an hour and after they shook hands with us they went away. Kept good watch all night, not trusting them. The weather was disagreeable.

SUNDAY, FEBRUARY 10,1793.

At half past five in the morning set out, the wind ahead; at ten o'clock passed Hermitage Island; was obliged to encamp at 11 o'clock, not being able to travel because of the force of the wind; remained encamped all day. Traveled three leagues in the morning.

MONDAY, FEBRUARY 11, 1793.

Started at half past five. The wind being favorable, put up the sail; landed at noon. At 4 o'clock in the evening passed a barge laden with salted meat which came from the Belle Riviere; at half past five encamped on the east bank. Traveled six leagues and a half. The weather overcast with rain and very cold.

TUESDAY, FEBRUARY 12, 1793.

Sleet fell all night. The wind very strong from the northeast and growing very cold. Was not able to journey until noon when the wind calmed somewhat and the weather cleared a little fairer. While we were on land, a barge which was drifing on the river passed on the other side. At 3 o'clock passed around an island on the west side; at 5 o'clock encamped on the upper point of the island. Traveled three leagues.

WEDNESDAY, FEBRUARY 13, 1793.

At half past five resumed our journey, the wind calm and the weather very cold. At 10 o'clock passed the little meadow where there was an abandoned house. It seemed to me that maize had been grown. This meadow is on the west bank. It is not under water. It lies alongside the river for a quarter of a league and extends in the depth of the lands; at 11 o'clock passed the mouth of the St. Francis River. At the mouth there is an island which forms two entrances to the river. At five o'clock in the evening encamped three leagues away from the St. Francis River. The river rose two feet in twenty-four hours. The current is very strong. The river still carries ice, which makes it very cold for us.

THURSDAY, FEBRUARY 14, 1793.

At 5 o'clock in the morning started off sailing, the wind fresh and favorable. At 10 o'clock passed inside Great Council Island which shortened our route by 4 leagues. The said flat makes a great turn of five leagues when the river is quite shallow. At noon there passed a barge which drifted on the river. I called to the man in charge to land, but the current was so strong that it could not reach the shore. I did not go out to it because it would have made me lose headway. I asked him where he came from. He replied that he came from Kentucky, that he was laden with tobacco, and that the owner of the barge was named Brouyain. The river is still filled with much ice and driftwood. Encamped on the inner side of an island at half past five. Appearance of bad weather. Made 9 leagues. All night the weather very disagreeable with thunder and hail.

FRIDAY, FEBRUARY 15, 1793.

The weather continues bad. At 10 o'clock set out; at noon passed some rapids so strong that we were hardly able to pass with all the oars and the sail. The wind was very fresh. The whole barge shook. By 2 o'clock the weather became so bad that I was obliged to encamp in the shelter of an island. Traveled 3 leagues. By midnight the weather was severe because of the force of the wind and rain; and the earth was falling on the bank opposite to us.

SATURDAY, FEBRUARY 16, 1793.

All day the wind and rain very high, unable to travel. The river rose 4 feet in scarcely 24 hours. The river still filled with ice and the temperature very cold.

SUNDAY, FEBRUARY 17, 1793.

We set out at 6 o'clock in the morning, the weather calm, still overcast; at 10 o'clock passed on the inside of an island near the west shore; at 3 o'clock passed on the inside of an island near the east bank; at half past five encamped on a point above the said island. Ice continually passed. Made five and a half leagues during the day. The weather overcast.

MONDAY, FEBRUARY 18, 1793.

Set out at half past five in the morning with high winds ahead and fog; at 10 o'clock passed on the inside of an island on the east side. The river was filled with wood. At 5 o'clock encamped on the point of an island which is in the middle of the river. Made 4 leagues. There was rain and thunder all night. The river rose 2 feet.

TUESDAY, FEBRUARY 19, 1793.

The weather was terrible all day with rain and thunder. Remained encamped the entire day, being unable to travel. The river rose 2 feet in 24 hours. The current was very swift.

WEDNESDAY, FEBRUARY 20, 1793.

At half past five continued the route, the weather clearing up. Passed on the right side of the island where we encamped. At 8 o'clock saw the beginning of the Ecors a Margot below which there is a bayou, or little river. It flows through the land which separates the low land from the high. At 9 o'clock we were at the point of the island. At the left of the island there is another island. At the same hour saw three barges which were drifting. I called to them to land. They landed at the bluff. I went across to them. Two were coming from Cumberland, loaded with wheat, and the other was coming from Kentucky laden with salted meat. All three were going to New Orleans. Needing meat for my company, I bought from the barge master a hundred pounds of pork at 10 piastres, which satisfied him, and gave to him a letter for Monsieur the governor of Natchez. He told me that there was no news from above or from the United States of America. I continued my journey at 10 o'clock. The wind being favorable, I put up the sail. At 11 o'clock I was across the Ecors a Margot. At noon I had passed the Margot River which is the termination of said Ecors a Margot. At 1 o'clock the wind had calmed. I landed on an island to prepare dinner. Started on at 3 o'clock. Passed several islands. At half past five camped on an island in the middle of the river. The weather fine all night. Made 6 leagues.

THURSDAY, FEBRUARY 21, 1793.

Set out at half past five, the weather serene; passed several islands in the middle of the river; at noon, landed for dinner. Set out again at 2 o'clock. At half past five in the evening encamped above the Thousand Islands on the last island upon a point near the east bank. The place bears this name because of the number of islands located on a point of the eastern bank. Traveled 5 leagues during the day, the weather fine, the wind calm. In the evening caught a brill which two men could not carry because of its enormous size.

FRIDAY, FEBRUARY 22,1793.

Got under way at half past five in the morning. The wind, a fresh gale, being favorable, I set the sail; at 10 passed several islands near the west bank; at noon landed for dinner. Resumed the journey at 2 o'clock; at 3 passed several islands on the west side; at half past five encamped at the foot of Devil's Island which bears this name because of the force of the current which is encountered there in passing it and the number of stumps present there. Made 6 leagues.

SATURDAY, FEBRUARY 23, 1793.

Set out at half past five in the morning. At half past nine doubled Devil's Island, fell to the leeward half a league from the second bluff which is very high and named the Ecors a Prudhomme. A fresh gale began to blow up from the south. Put up the sail. At half past twelve we doubled the third bluff which is very high and the river there is very narrow. It is three leagues from the second bluff to the third. Did not land for dinner, the wind being good. At 4 o'clock passed a large island in the middle of the river. At half past five encamped above the fourth bluff, a distance of three leagues from the third, which one finds on the river after passing the Ecors a Margot. The weather was overcast, with the appearance of rain and bad weather. We moored very securely in a bayou at the end of the fourth Ecors. Made 9 leagues.

SUNDAY, FEBRUARY 24, 1793.

The weather was bad all night with rain. The rain continued all day with the wind very cool from the northeast. Unable to start, we remained encamped all day. The river rose 2 feet in 24 hours. The river was filled with swiftly-drifting obstructions. I went ashore despite the rain to see the land of the bluff. It is very level when one is three arpents inland and did not appear to me very good. The trees are under water, white and red oaks, hickory, and other wood which I do not know.

MONDAY, FEBRUARY 25, 1793.

The weather was disagreeable all night. Sleet and snow fell. The wind from the northwest is very high. It rained hard and thundered all day. It was not possible for us to travel; remained in camp.

TUESDAY, FEBRUARY 26, 1793.

It rained all night and all day. It has not been possible for us to leave. Remained encamped. The river twice rose three feet in twenty-four hours. The day before one of my men asked me if he could go hunting to kill a deer and he has not yet reappeared. I sent two men into the woods to see if they could find him and fired several gunshots and shots from the swivel gun to see if he replied, but heard nothing. The men I sent returned and found neither him nor his tracks.

WEDNESDAY, FEBRUARY 27, 1793.

The weather has cleared. I again sent some men into the woods and fired several shots from the swivel guns, but he did not reply. At noon my company returned from the woods, telling me that they saw nothing. I left food enough for him for several days at the encampment, hung a handkerchief from a tree so that, in case he returned to the same encampment, he would go to an Indian encampment which we left 2 leagues below where we were. Set out at noon, with the wind ahead. I traveled three leagues. I saw three barges tied up to the west bank as the sun was setting. I crossed over and encamped with them. I found that they all belonged to Mr. Du Paw, loaded with tobacco and salted meat going to New Orleans. The proprietor had a passport from Monsieur the Baron de Carondelet, governor general of this province. There were also several French families who were going down with him from Gallipolis in America. They came to settle in this province. I gave to Mr. Du Paw, proprietor of the barges, a letter for Monsieur the governor of Natchez in which was included a copy of the speech which the half-breed Chickasaw made to me. I asked the ovner of the barge, if he saw a man on the bank of the river, to send for him and I told him that I had lost a man who went hunting. The two barges gave me no news. Traveled two leagues.

THURSDAY, FEBRUARY 28, 1793.

At six o'clock in the morning the barges cleared the shore and I set sail with the wind ahead in a fresh gale and very cold. Both banks of the river were frozen. At 10 o'clock the wind was so high that I was obliged to land, not being able to travel. At 4 o'clock the wind calmed a little. I set out and at 6 o'clock in the evening encamped on the second Canadian Island. Made 3 leagues.

FRIDAY, MARCH 1, 1793.

Left camp at 6 o'clock in the morning, the weather overcast, the wind calm, but looking like snow, being very cold. At noon prepared dinner at the mouth of the Bayone River on the west bank. Encamped at 6 o'clock above Canadian Islands which are seven in number. Came 6 leagues.

SATURDAY, MARCH 2, 1793.

It rained all night until 8 o'clock when the sky cleared. I set out, the wind calm. At noon I landed to prepare dinner. While we were at dinner, a pirogue passed on the other side. The river was so wide that we were unable to speak to it. Set sail at 2 o'clock, with the weather serene; at 6 o'clock encamped on the west bank. Traveled 5 leagues; passed three islands on the same shore, passed on the inside.

SUNDAY, MARCH 3, 1793.

At 2 o'clock in the morning there was a terrible landslide. The trees fell on all sides, which obliged us to break camp and go half a league in the night. We moored to the land waiting for day-light. The Mississippi began to overflow everywhere. Started at half past five; passed two islands on the left side, landed at noon. The wind being favorable, we set sail; at half past six encamped in a little meadow 10 leagues from New Madrid. The land was very high and not under water. It might be 8 arpents in extent and the trees around are oaks. Since it was quite late when I arrived there, I could not see well. I left that for my return. Made 6 leagues. My company made a fire on the prairie in the morning upon leaving. In an instant it was all on fire.

MONDAY, MARCH 4, 1793.

Set out at 6 o'clock in the morning, the weather overcast, bad weather threatening. At noon the weather was very bad with much rain. I landed on the inside of an island and encamped on the east side. The rain fell all day. At 6 o'clock in the evening the wind shifted to the north in a fresh gale. Traveled 3 leagues in the morning. Found the current very swift.

TUESDAY, MARCH 5, 1793.

Started at 6 o'clock in the morning, the wind ahead, very high, the weather clear. At 10 o'clock as we doubled the island on the west side, there passed in the cove two barges which were drifting, but they were too far away to speak to them. Encamped at half past six on an island on the west side. Traveled 4 leagues. The weather was fair, the wind calm.

WEDNESDAY, MARCH 6, 1793.

Resumed our journey at 6 o'clock, the weather fair, the wind good; at 8 o'clock saw the Fort of New Madrid at a distance of one and a half leagues; at 10 o'clock moored before the said fort. I delivered to the commandant, Don Thomas Portell, the packet from the governor general of this province and those from the governor of the town of Natchez and apprised him of my mission. Delivered over the three soldiers who came to complete his garrison and who came on board at Natchez. Found at the wharf of said post a schooner of about 55 tons without mast which arrived from the Belle Riviere loaded with maize belonging to Doctor Water, an inhabitant of the said post, who was going to ship a mast in order to go down to New Orleans next April. There was an American barge laden with pelts coming from Cas in Illinois, having on board three French passengers who were going from the United States to New Orleans. The names of the three Frenchmen — the Chevalier de Luziere, from Allegheny County, Mr. Barthelemy Tardiveau of Kaskaskia, Illinois, Guy Bryan, merchant of Philadelphia, and Pierre Audrain of Fort Pitt, all in the states of America.

THURSDAY, MARCH 7, 1793.

There was rain and sleet all day. The rain fell and froze as it fell. The weather very cold, the wind very high from the northeast. At 10 o'clock in the evening the snow fell hard.

FRIDAY, MARCH 8, 1793.

The weather very gloomy, the wind very strong from the northwest. There were 6 inches of snow on the ground. At noon the weather had cleared. It continued clear all day, but very cold.

SATURDAY, MARCH 9,1793.

The weather fair and moderate. I unloaded the two guns of eight and all the implements of war, which I had for the post and which I brought to the commandant. At noon I observed the height of the sun. I found by my observation that the fort of New Madrid is in the latitude of 36 degrees 8 minutes north and its longitude is 93 degrees 15 minutes, having corrected the distance from the horizon. The barge from Kaskaskia has cleared port for New Orleans.

SUNDAY, MARCH 10, 1793.

The weather is overcast and rainy, the wind from the northeast in a fresh gale. The commandant reviewed the militia of his post which totals 130 infantrymen and 20 gunners. He gave recognition to a captain, a lieutenant, and a second lieutenant to whom I brought commissions from the governor general of this province, the Baron de Carondelet. The commandant and the captain of the militia told me that he still lacked many men who had not yet returned from trading, and that they were able to make up 180 men in this post. They are all French and German with the exception of twenty Americans, English, and Irish. It rained all day, the weather very bad and very cold, the wind very high.

MONDAY, MARCH 11, 1793.

The weather quite fine, but very cold. At 10 o'clock in the morning the commandant sent for the Loup chiefs to talk to them about the barge which some men of their nation had destroyed at the Ecors a Margot. They replied that they would send them immediately, that they would deliver them to the said commandant, that he could do whatever he wished with them, but that surely they had taken them for some Americans, for they did not think that there was a man in their nation who wished to harm either the Spaniards or the French, that every day they told their young men that we were all their brothers, and that they had no father but the King of Spain. They said also that their entire nation was going to come this summer to form a village on the Grand Prairie, 6 leagues distant from New Madrid, that they were in numbers between eight and nine hundred warriors and many women and children.

The same day I mounted a horse with the commandant to see the environs of New Madrid. At a quarter of a league from the fort there is a prairie which extends upwards to Illinois and downwards to the St. Francis River. The prairie is about one league wide in this place and extends to a very wide lake named Ste. Marie; and on the other side of the lake it is still prairie land. On leaving the fort and the site of the village of New Madrid where there are several houses built which are beginning to form streets, and entering the prairie one finds a little Cherokee village of three families and with them their chief named Lean Bear. On the edge of the prairie there are several inhabitants at 6 arpents distance from each other. The soil of the prairie is very good and black. It is necessary to dig 5 feet to find gravel. Wheat grows there very abundantly and corn, potatoes, and oats grow very well. The whole prairie is at present covered with strawberry plants. The whole prairie is covered with

66

plum trees, apple trees, and other wild fruits of the country. The animals of the prairie are very fat. On the Lake Ste. Marie there is a superb cypress grove from where one is able to get much cypress for building, but the cypress is not used for making stakes for fences. The inhabitants surround their sown fields with posts of sassafras, oak, and white ash, but they do not last.

TUESDAY, MARCH 12, 1793.

The wind is from the northwest, the weather clear. The savage chiefs of the Shawnees, Loups, Cherokees, and Ottawas made known to me through the interpreter that they would like to go for a sail with me on the Mississippi in the galiot La Fleche. At 2 o'clock in the afternoon they embarked with the commandant of New Madrid, Don Thomas Portell. I saluted them with seven shots from the swivel guns which appeared to please them immensely.

I went up one league above New Madrid and came down on the other side through the channel of the island which is opposite New Madrid and emerged a half a league below the fort of New Madrid. Beyond cannon range there is a large body of water where all sorts of craft may pass, but, as large as it is, when the river is low the channel is dried up. There are actually 30 feet of water in the said channel. Several lighters, barges, and conveyances have already passed which did not stop at New Madrid, because they entered into this channel without being seen, since its mouth is not seen from New Madrid and when they are below, they are already too far away and descend without anyone knowing where they come from, or that they are at New Madrid. It will be very easy to obstruct this pass in the middle of the said island.

There is in the channel another little island where the passage on each side is not more than 30 or 40 feet wide which becomes actually dry when the river is low. I think one could easily obstruct this passage by planting the soil with willow trees and creepers at a certain distance from each other which would stop the driftwood and would in a short time form a considerable impediment which it would be impossible to pass even with pirogues. There is another higher short cut, but it is entirely obstructed by impediments and one cannot even pass with pirogues. This short cut comes out below the said island and enters a half a league higher. On the east bank opposite the point above the said island, there is another short cut which emerges 4 leagues up the river. We returned to New Madrid at 6 o'clock in the evening. I again saluted the savage chiefs with seven more shots from the swivel gun to prove to them the pleasure which they had given me by accompanying me on this sail in the ship of my great King.

WEDNESDAY, MARCH 13, 1793.

The weather fair, I prepared to descend. At 10 o'clock in the morning, being at the house of the commandant, the chief of the Shawnees with the notables of his village came to talk with the said commandant. One who spoke good English addressed me and indicated that they would like to have among them one of those who knew how to speak Spanish in order not to be always deceived by white men who imposed upon them, never reporting to them things as they are nor the same words that their Spanish father said to them. He also said that at the time of the English there had been one of their nation who spoke and wrote English and, when the King of England wished to send them some message, he wrote them and he who knew how to read English read it to the whole nation; and when they wished to send word to the King of England, he wrote it and so they knew the truth. But when the messages have to go through the lips of interpreters who often say to them what they wish and often do not report the same words that the chiefs say to their father, it prevents their father from knowing what their intentions are towards the Spaniards.

I replied to him that, if they wished to give me a young man on condition that I take him away to my great chief of New Orleans who would regard him as a son and have him taught how to speak our language and that afterwards he would return to their village, I would do it. They reflected a moment, and the oldest said to me "My brother, if you will not leave for three days, I shall go where the great chief was and the great chief and all the councillors, who were 16 leagues above at the mouth of the Belle Riviere, shall decide whether or not to send the young man and, if they do not decide to send him, I shall return in three days." He then requested me to wait these three days. I promised him and he left at once. The others remained at New Madrid awaiting his return.

THURSDAY, MARCH 14, 1793.

All day the weather has been quite fair, the wind cold. Nothing remarkable has happened. The celebrated fort of New Madrid is square with four bastions which are northeast and southwest. Two bastions are erected on the river with two cannon of six, one of four, and a swivel gun. The fort has a house within to accommodate the commandant. It is 50 feet long and 20 feet wide, with a gallery, 10 feet wide on three sides. There are quarters, 80 feet long by 20 feet wide in which there is a storehouse for the artillery supplies, a storehouse for provisions, 40 feet long and 20 feet wide, a powder magazine, 10 feet square, a hospital, 20 feet long by 12 feet wide, a dungeon, 16 feet long and 11 wide divided in two, a bakehouse, 15 feet long and 12 feet wide, a guardhouse, 16 feet long and 11 feet wide, and an outbuilding, 10 feet long and 5 wide. The fort is 2312 feet around, and is enclosed by posts five inches in thickness and by a moat 15 feet wide and 6 deep over which there is a bridge in front of the fort, 13 feet in width with two rails, and a parapet, enclosed by 2 inch posts. The fort is 250 feet from the Mississippi. The land has been under water much of the time since the fort has been built, but they tell me that the river has not overflowed for some time.

FRIDAY, MARCH 15,1793.

The weather very bad with rain, the wind blowing a fresh gale from the south. At 10 o'clock in the morning a barge arrived from the post of Vincennes on the Wabash River. It told us nothing new. All was very peaceful at the headquarters of the Americans, and the Americans were making every effort to make peace with the savages. These same men of the barge told us that they were not successful, and that the savages kill all the Americans they find on the Belle Riviere. They told us that the Americans had resolved to march against the savages this summer, if they did not make peace with them. They do not seem to fear them and are preparing to receive them.

SATURDAY, MARCH 16, 1793.

The weather is bad with a great deal of rain, the wind very high from south. I took my provisions on board and prepared to depart when the savages should arrive. The same weather continued all day, much rain.

SUNDAY, MARCH 17, 1793.

The weather rainy and wind from the south, a fresh gale. Expecting the savages any minute, prepared to set out adrift for Natchez. At noon the weather very bad, with rain and hail. At midnight the wind drifted to the north, very cool, and snow fell until Monday morning.

MONDAY, MARCH 18, 1793.

Very strong wind from the north. The weather has cleared; still expecting the savages and determined to start tomorrow, if they do not arrive, because they promised to return last Saturday; and it seems to us that they have decided not to send the young man of whom they spoke, but in order to show them that I trust them I have remained three days longer than I promised to wait, being ready to leave.

TUESDAY, MARCH 19,1793.

The day fair, the wind southward, a little cool. Seeing that the savages had not arrived, I sent for the interpreter to find out what was keeping them. He replied that they had, perhaps, gone farther to hunt and that they would be several days yet returning. As the water was high they would not come immediately. Therefore I decided to depart and arranged with Don Thomas Portell, commandant of said post, that if they were of the same mind, they should come to New Orleans. Immediately, I fired a shot from the swivel gun and called my company. I took leave of the commandant. He intrusted me with a packet for the governor general and one for the governor of Natchez. He also entrusted me with Medard Mitchel, an American, to take to the Governor and with a map of the waters of the Mississippi by the said Medard Mitchel. I left at half past eight. At noon I arrived at Little Prairie. When I went on land I found that the shore was still two and a half feet higher than the water. The land extends high half a league above and a league below. A pretty settlement could be made there. At one league from the Prairie inland there is a bayou which empties into the St. Francis River and goes upwards nearly to New Madrid. The lands on the other side of the bayou are all hillocks and are never under water, so one of the hunters of New Madrid told me who is there every day. One could establish a beautiful settlement there. It is very close to the Arkansas. Cleared the shore at 2 o'clock; noted all the points and islands in order to make a map of the river; at 7 o'clock in the evening moored on one of the Canadian Islands, not finding any land as all the land has been flooded since we left the little prairie. Traveled 23 leagues during the day.

WEDNESDAY, MARCH 20, 1793.

Set out at 5 o'clock in the morning. At 9 o'clock passed the Ecors a Farine. Landed at the place where we lost the man to see whether he did not return. We did not find the sea biscuit we left in a handkerchief in the tree which makes me think that he returned and may have made a cageux or that he may have been taken by the small boats which descend the river. At 11 o'clock we passed the Ecors a Prudhomme; at noon passed in the center, noticing always the points and islands and their distances; at 7 o'clock in the evening moored to some willows, not being able to find any shore. All the land of both banks is inundated. I have only seen land at the Ecors. Traveled 24 leagues today. The wind southwards, a little cool. The weather fair.

THURSDAY, MARCH 21, 1793.

Started at 5 o'clock in the morning; at 7 o'clock landed at the mouth of the river of the Ecors a Margot. I went on land immediately with six men to hunt. I found near the mouth of the River a Margot a wonderful place to make a fortification. The land had an elevation of 50 feet and was not flooded. There is a little flat below which protects the mouth of the river and extends above and below along the Mississippi. There are two immense trees on one of which is written Jaime a Kin, April 9, 1791, and on the other Tomas, April 9, 1791. I surveyed the land for a league around. One can see little more than beautiful lands in some places consisting of little hills and in others, all flat. On the river there are many cypress trees for building. Plums, hazel nuts, and chestnut trees are very common. There are many ash trees, a number of oaks, walnut trees, sassafras, and many other trees. There are many springs in the interior. The land seemed to me to be very good. I went on board again at half past ten. I set sail immediately. At 11 o'clock passed the river, below the Ecors a Margot, which is found at the entrance of the Ecors. It is very navigable and by it one can go to the other river in a very short time. At 4 o'clock passed Council Shoals. At half past six passed the St. Francis River. All the land submerged since we left the Ecors a Margot. We did not find any land only the little prairie a league below the St. Francis River where we camped. The land was still three feet higher than the river from which it appeared to me that it was never submerged. Made 35 leagues in the day.

FRIDAY, MARCH 22, 1793.

Sailed at 5 o'clock in the morning, the wind at the prow, a fresh gale. At 9 o'clock passed the Hermitage. At noon it began to rain. From the prairie to the White River the land of both banks was submerged. At 5 o'clock at night landed on an island at the mouth of the White River. Delivered to the sergeant of the Arkansas detachment the letters for his commandant which Don

Thomas Portell, commandant of New Madrid, gave me. The said sergeant told me that a barge which was going down had found the man I lost at the Ecors and that the two I left ill at the Arkansas had departed with the same barge. Immediately, I put off from shore. At 7 o'clock I moored to some willows, not being able to find land to camp. Made 28 leagues.

SATURDAY, MARCH 23, 1793.

Sailed at 5 o'clock in the morning; at 7 o'clock passed the mouth of the Arkansas River; at noon passed the 3 channels at 8 leagues from the Arkansas; at 2 o'clock passed the channels at twelve leagues; at 3 o'clock passed a superb cypress grove on the east bank; afterwards passed land a league and a half long, very high, which was three feet above the water; landed to see if it was not innunduated at high water. There were no marks visible on the trees to indicate that it was ever submerged. The reeds did not hinder me from penetrating inland. Immediately after starting on, I passed the Isle aux Chicots. Below the island on the east side there is a league of land which is not submerged. It is not nearly so high as the first. At 7 o'clock moored to some willows on the east side. Have not found any land except in the places mentioned. Made 27 leagues today. The wind still ahead and fresh. In the night the weather was terrible with wind and rain. The billows and the wind were so high that I was obliged to cross over to shelter myself from the wind and waves. Crossed at midnight; moored to some trees, no land.

SUNDAY, MARCH 24, 1793.

At 6 o'clock in the morning the wind was favorable and quite calm; at noon passed Death's Head Island. At 2 o'clock passed three islands on the west side; at 4 o'clock passed 4 islands on the east side; at 6 o'clock passed one large and one small island on the west side; at half past six passed 6 islands on the same side; at 7 o'clock landed on a ridge of land on the west bank, but all the land was submerged. The land which I passed was submerged on both sides all day. Traveled 38 leagues.

73

MONDAY, MARCH 25, 1793.

Sailed at 5 o'clock in the morning, the wind ahead; at 7 o'clock passed the land of a large island on the west side. On dry ground there is a league of land, which was not flooded, at 3 leagues from the Yazoo River; at seven o'clock passed the Yazoo River; at half past eight arrived at the Fort of Nogales. Not finding any letters from my chiefs, I set out for Natchez; observed all islands and points; at 7 o'clock in the evening passed the Grand Gulf; at 10 o'clock the small one. The moon was very clear which favored me for my observations. At midnight it became to very dark that I was obliged to moor to some willows until daylight when I set sail; at 6 o'clock in the morning moored at Natchez. I went immediately to the governor of the town to whom I rendered account of my mission and delivered the packets which the commandant of New Madrid, Don Thomas Portell, intrusted to me.

NEW MADRID ON THE MISSISSIPPI WAS A THRIVING CENTER DURING THE SPANISH REGIME IN LOUISIANA.

Comments on Rousseau's Voyage

The following excerpts from a letter written by Manuel Gayoso de Lemos to the Baron de Carondelet show that Rousseau's services to the colony were not ignored.

Natchez, April 4, 1793

I have already informed your Lordship of the return to this post of Captain Don Pedro Rousseau, and I herewith transmit in addition, the diary of his journey which he gave me, accompanied by a map of the river from this post to Nuevo Madrid, and a second of the said post of Nuevo Madrid, and a third of the Barrancas de Margo, since part of the river between the said heights is of great importance. (It is usually considered that this refers to Wolf River and another smaller stream near the present Memphis, but the description more probably refers to the Big Hatchee and Obion or Forked Deer)....

In addition to the statement of the diary I will add the verbal report which Don Pedro Rousseau has given me with reference the Barrancas de Margo. . . .

The Barrancas de Margo rise in front of the Island of El Diemanta at the mouth of the river Carondelet. By sailing along the bank two leagues to the north one comes upon the river Las Casas. These rivers had no names, and are those commonly known indiscriminately as the river Des Ecors a Margo. . . . For all points I refer to the diary.

I am unable to pass over in silence the credit which I regard as due the making of the maps of the river. It is wonderful that in so few days as were taken by his voyage from Nuevo Madrid to this post, Don Pedro Rousseau should have marked out the directions and distances so accurately that they agreed with the observed latitudes and longitudes. I am perfectly certain that the work is entirely his own without his having been guided by a model, for there is none in existence with the details with which he has made his map. . . .

Don Pedro Rousseau, in my opinion, deserves special credit for his fulfillment of his commission. I can do no less than call it to your Lordship's attention, so that by adding this to the other considerations which recommend him, you may be pleased to make use of them all for the benefit of his promotion.

In a letter to Carondelet Rousseau said that the militiamen of New

Madrid were kept faithful only by stopping up holes to their cellars to keep them from hiding.

(Rousseau to Carondelet on board the galley La Venganza)

(Privateers of the Guadaloupe, the La. Qua., April 1940, vol. 23)

Rousseau wrote Carondelet that many of the subjects residing in New Madrid were Americans who were not generally influenced by the "French revolutionary precepts," that at no time could the militia of the upper valley be depended upon entirely for a vigorous defense against their countrymen.

The plan of invading Louisiana from the American West probably originated with George Rogers Clark and his associates before the outbreak of war between France and Spain. . . . In December 1792, Clark apparently sent his first suggestions to France relative to a campaign against Louisiana. His brother-in-law, James O'Fallon, later wrote to a friend that Clark had discussed the plan with him "last Christmas" and that he had "framed the whole of the correspondence in the General's name" and corroborated it by a private letter to Thomas Paine, who was then a member of the Convention in France. Paine's reply dated February 17, 1793, seemed to indicate that the matter had been brought before the Provisory Executive Council by Edmund Genet, the newly appointed minister to the United States, before his departure for America. When Genet arrived in Philadelphia he found a detailed plan of the campaign which Clark had forwarded. Clark claimed that he could "raise 1500 brave men or thereabouts" in American frontier settlements, and as many more from the French in Spanish Illinois and the Americans at Natchez. He predicted that, if the French fleet could cut off Spanish reinforcements, Louisiana and West Florida would quickly be taken. — Lawrence Kinnaird, "Spain in the Mississippi Valley."

Friendly Indians

In this same letter de Lemos tells of the deals he made with the Indians, such as getting their permission to build a fort, and "talking them out of land;" that is, refusing to pay them for the land he needed, or when he did pay them it was a small amount. He invited several of the Indian chiefs to dine with him and Don Pedro Rousseau, and after the meal, which apparently pleased them well, they agreed to give him the land on which to build a fort free of any cost. The leader of these Indians was Ugulayacabe, who took a fancy to Rousseau and assured him that he could build the fort under his protection. He kept his word, for de Lemos says in his letter: "This morning at day break I sent fifty men in charge of Don Pedro Rousseau, who came back at noon to eat, the work having advanced greatly without opposition."

The Redmen admired Rousseau for his bravery. When he established Fort San Fernando (in 1795) at what was then known as Ecores des Margot, the Chickasaw Indians, seeing that he cleared the land with his men all unarmed, were greatly pleased and sent word to de Lemos through their chief, Ugulayacabe, that they would like to give him the name of "Payemingo," meaning without fear.

Gayoso de Lemos, with the assistance of Rousseau, had made a good deal with these Indians at Esperanza on the Las Casas River; he acquired 3,000 arpents of land for a good meal and flattering phrases. But he was after all a man of honor, and to show his gratitude for the Indians' generosity he gave them forty-one Indian shirts, nine barrels of brandy, ninety pounds of powder, sixty balls, one hundred flint-lock muskets, and food for their voyage, which was about four or five miles from this place to their village.

Vol. 25, La. Hist. Quarterly

Spies and Pirates

Gayoso and Rousseau were called upon to assume the entire responsibility for keeping the colony free of spies, and also the lakes, the river, and the gulf free of pirates. They were during the administration of Carondelet the most active officers in Louisiana, and they worked well together, for they had formed a close friendship, and both spoke English and Spanish with equal facility. (Gayoso had been educated in England.) Of all the pirates and spies General William Augustus Bowles was the most troublesome. Among them also was Medad Mitchel, who caused considerable excitement, for, as Bowles, he was exceedingly clever.

Medad Mitchel had the good fortune to be taken at the age of fifteen under the protection of Friedrich Wilhelm, Baron von Steuben, the Prussian general in the American Revolution, who treated him as his own son, and gave him a military education. After the War he was employed as a surveyor for the state of New York but soon gave up this position and became successively agent, commissary, and chief surveyor for the Scioto Company, in which he held some shares of stock. This enterprise was in the real estate business as well as in trading, and he held large stretches of land in the western part of Illinois close to the Missouri line, not far from New Madrid, near the mouth of the Scioto River, which was purchased on credit and sold for cash at high prices to people in Europe (especially in France) who wished to settle in America. A town, Gallipolis, was established by the Company, and many Europeans who had immigrated there on promises of fertile land which would grow any kind of crop found a mere wilderness totally unsuited for cultivation and lost their investments. Farmers in the vicinity said that the land was not worth ten cents an acre. It was Count de Barthe who proposed the settlement of Gallipolis, and Colonel William Duer, the Company's president, managed the affairs. Many of the immigrants, having lost all, were compelled to move to other villages and seek employment. A number of French royalist families had settled there but became dissatisfied and moved to a location two miles from Ste. Genevieve, which they called New Bourbon. It was a beautiful spot, located on a hill overlooking a valley which led to the Mississippi River not far away.

When the company was on the verge of failure, Mitchel was commissioned to sail in a pilot boat, with the greatest possible expedition, from New York to England, in order to reach there before the post with the news of the impending failure of the company, to negotiate the acceptance of fifty thousand pesos of bills of exchange drawn by the Society of Manufacturers against the Scioto Company. He fulfilled this commission in England but upon his return to New York found that the promises made him were not to be kept, and this made him very angry. For spite he resolved to destroy the settlement of Gallipolis, and set out for that village to carry out his purpose.

He succeeded in persuading many of the inhabitants to move to New Madrid, and in some cases offered to pay their expense of moving (but Gayoso says he did not keep his promises, for he was not able to do so). He established himself in New Madrid, and besides continuing his effort to ruin Gallipolis seemed to have no special object or interest whatsoever. Don Tomas Portel, the commandant at New Madrid, became suspicious of him, and had him carefully watched by his lieutenants. Presently he was dicovered making a copy of the map of the Mississippi which Rousseau had made, and Portel promptly had him arrested, and sent him to Natchez where Gayoso and Rousseau were stationed.

When he arrived Gayoso questioned him at length concerning his reason for making a copy of the map. He answered that he was only practicing at map-making, and had no idea of selling information to any other nation. Obviously this young man had been reared a gentleman, and Gayoso invited him to spend a week at his palatial home, Concord, and although he was a guest continued to question him in the hope that he would inadvertently reveal his secret, if he had one. But

Mitchel was too clever for that. Finally Rousseau announced that his ship was ready to sail to New Orleans, and Gayoso decided to send Mitchel to Carondelet.

WILLIAM AUGUSTUS BOWLES

There he stood. A white gladiator in the best tradition. One of his Spanish foes had once written his superiors about the man who made the southeastern United States vibrate with unconcealed glory: "The height of Mr. Bowles attracts our attention because of its size and the shape of his body, which is similar to that of the famous ancient gladiators, filled as it is with force and activity." The writer went on to denigrate Bowles in no uncertain terms: "He is skilled in several arts—he is an actor without ever having appeared in more than three shows in his life; a painter without his canvases having attracted any attention; a chemist who lacks the basic knowledge; a sailor who knows not the arts of navigation."

Whatever the snide remarks of his detractors, William Augustus Bowles was a formidable man. For a decade he kept the Spanish-American frontier in a turmoil. And his nemesis was the Spanish governor at New Orleans, the Baron de Carondelet. The man who was appointed to bring Bowles to his untimely end was Rousseau.

When Bowles and his Seminole allies captured the store of the Scottish firm of Panton, Leslie and Company at San Marcos de Apalache (St. Marks, Florida), the Spanish officials were clearly worried. But when Bowles declared all Florida ports open to free world commerce, the mercantilistic Spaniards were really amazed! Here was a native-born Marylander, now the self-styled "Director of the Muscogee Nation," who threatened Spanish hegemony in the Gulf of Merico. "No way," said Carondelet, as he sent his director of the port of New Orleans, José de Hevia, in cooperation with Rousseau, to capture Bowles. The success of that expedition owes much to the skill and genius of Rousseau.

80

General William Augustus Bowles
Captured by Rousseau

General William Augustus Bowles, a native of Maryland, was born October 22, 1763. He was a Loyalist, and said that he hated the United States because he and his family had suffered untold humiliation and financial ruin at the hands of the Americans. He enlisted in the British army in 1776, and the following year was commissioned an ensign and sent to Pensacola. He had not been there long before he was disciplined for insubordination, whereupon in a fit of anger he threw off his uniform and tendered his resignation, which was accepted without argument, for he was too vain and troublesome to be of much use. He then went away with some Indians and enjoyed their hospitality. He was, however, too ambitious for a life of idleness. After a few months he returned and again joined the British, army but as he was not amenable to discipline he was soon dismissed. After a long spell of loafing he found himself destitute, and made a boat out of a hogshead, and using a blanket for a sail, cruised along the shore of the Bay of Pensacola, living on game and fish. But when winter came he persuaded a baker at Pensacola to take him in. There he enjoyed the comforts of a well-ordered home but since he would not work for his keep he was requested to leave. He then joined his Indian friends, and in 1781, when the Spanish attacked Pensacola, he led a body of Indians to assist the British forces but when the Spanish were on the verge of victory he put on his ensign uniform so as to be classified as a prisoner of war, and was shipped to Brooklyn with some British troops and held there. But he escaped and somehow acquired a schooner in which he sailed to New Providence, took another man's wife and went on to St. Augustine. From there he went to the Bahamas, where he became an actor, an art in which he was moderately successful although he had no previous training. His versatility was remarkable. He gave up acting and became a portrait painter. He was skilful enough in this work to make a living. Being of a restless disposition, he soon abandoned this trade, and abandoned also the woman with whom he escaped from New Providence.

MARRIES AN INDIAN PRINCESS

He then met Lord Dunmore, governor of the Bahamas, and won his friendship. His attractive personality and plausible manner impressed the governor, and he appointed him agent of a trading post in West Florida. But as soon as he was settled among the Indians he married the daughter of one of the Creek chiefs, and suggested to them that under his leadership they could destroy the Spanish power in West Florida. He told them that the goods in the various trading posts throughout the territory were really presents sent them (by the English) and wrongfully kept by the Spanish. He would see to it that they got what was rightfully theirs, especially the merchandise in the large stores of Panton, Leslie and Company at Fort St. Marks. They believed him and as proof of their confidence gave him the title of Director of Muskogee Nation.

In 1790 he went to England with a party of Indians, and received a hearty welcome from British officials in London. They entertained him royally and loaded him and the Indians with valuable gifts. They also employed Bowles, on a salary, to use his influence in enlisting the Indian tribes as England's allies.

He returned in 1791, and issued, January 4, 1792, the following proclamation:

Being appointed Director of the Affairs of the United Nation of the Creeks and Cherokee, I do hereby declare my intentions are to establish the free ingress and egress of the vessels of all Nations (not at war with us) to the Port & Rivers on this coast.

He then marched upon Fort St. Marks, and in a surprise attack seized the store of Panton, Leslie and Company, a firm which held a commercial monopoly from

Spain. But he did not hold the fort; the Spanish forces drove him out.

One objective was to create an independent Indian nation between the United States and Canada. Although he had resigned from the British service during the American Revolution, he was supported by leading British merchants. Luis de Las Casas, Captain General of Cuba, writing from Havana to Conde de Floridablanca, on April 21, 1792, said:

> "I cannot help being convinced that in both points he (Bowles) was aided and abetted by the English government in order to take possession of the commerce of the Southern Indians, and consequently the influence and direction of their operations as it has among the northern Indians by means of the retension of the fort which it should have transferred to the Americans by virtue of the last treaty of peace. Neither do I doubt that Bowles is a salaried emissary of the same government. The captain of a ship in the slave trade which in in this port affirms that Bowles receives a gratuity from the government of London, and he submitted evidence of certain amounts paid to Bowles, together with place and person from whom he received them. Captain Don Pedro Rousseau spoke to Bowles of this and he was unable to deny it. He confessed that for some time he had received it but afterwards considering it indecorous to receive a salary from a sovereign in whose service he no longer was, he had given it up. . . ."

CARONDELET RESORTS TO TRICKERY TO CAPTURE BOWLES. THIS IS DISAPPOINTING TO ROUSSEAU

Bowles then offered to negotiate a treaty between his newly formed Indian state and Spain. Carondelet, therefore, sent two officers, Jose de Hevia and Don Pedro Rousseau, to St. Marks with an invitation for him to come to New Orleans to discuss the matter and also a letter of safe conduct. Rousseau was not especially pleased to take part in this expedition, and was quite willing to let Jose de Hevia take the lead. He was averse to any sort of trickery (even the Indians had commented upon his fairness and courage), and he was aware that Carondelet was luring Bowles to New Orleans for a purpose other than to discuss the terms of a treaty.

Jose de Hevia was pleased to take the lead. He said in his "Diary concerning the Capture of William Bowles" (which is in possession of the Florida Historical Society):

> "I asked the Commander of the fort for troops which he could give me to accompany mine with Don Pedro Rousseau.
>
> "Don Pedro Rousseau translated for me statements concerning Bowles taking possession of store house since January 18 (Panton-Leslie Co's).
>
> "I loaded the grenadiers in one and Don Pedro Rousseau and myself in the other.
>
> "Concerning what happened since my departure from New Orleans on the commission which the Governor put me in charge with the command of the schooner 'la Galga,' His Majesty's packet boat which was taken provisionally, and armed with two 2-inch cannons; four 4-inch; two 3-inch; sixteen grenadiers from Louisiana, two commanders, a servant, a distinquido, the army Captain, Don Pedro Rousseau, three artillery men and a corporal."

This makes it clear that Carondelet was doubtful that Bowles would accept his "polite" invitation, and that he was to be taken by force if he refused. Las Casas, the Captain General at Havana, was of the impression that Bowles had been arrested in Florida, for in a letter to Floridablanca, under date of April 12, 1792, he said in part: "I approve the raise in salary for Don Pedro Rousseau after letting four or six months pass because it is to be paid to an individual who has served with distinction in the war and who, in this case, has performed promptly the duties which correspond to his position. He was responsible for Bowles, who was placed in his charge, and afterwards he was similarly responsible for him when he brought him from New Orleans to this place. I am not sufficiently acquainted with the merits and services of Don Joseph Hevia, but I find that on this occasion he proceeded with little circumspection in the manner of arresting Bowles."

Las Casas apparently did not approve of the manner in which Bowles was arrested, and laid the blame on Hevia, when, as a matter of fact, the scheme was conceived by Carondelet himself.

When Bowles arrived at New Orleans he assured Carondelet that he was not an enemy of Spain but only the United States. He admitted that he planned the destruction of Panton, Leslie & Company, for that firm, he said, could not be trusted; that it was exploiting the Indians and bringing the Spanish government into bad repute. He then suggested that the Creeks, Cherokees, Choctaws, and Chickasaws should unite with Spain to resist American attempts to appropriate their lands.

Bowles was well educated, very clever, if untrustworthy, and had a good command of English. In a letter which he wrote to the Creek chiefs before he left with Joseph de Hevia and Rousseau, he said: 'In consequence of the letter I wrote to the King and Ministers of Spain, the Governor of New Orleans has directions to settle in a peaceable way with this Nation a line of commerce upon this coast, for that reason the Governor has sent a vessel to conduct me to New Orleans, and has declared in his letter to me it is his intention to treat with me and to establish peace by doing away all falsehood that has so long plagued the chiefs and us all. I request therefore that the chiefs will rest quiet and take no steps that may create uneasiness until I return—for I shall consult the true interest of the Nation and not deviate from it . . . And it is My orders that no American subject come into the Nation until my return." He signed the letter "Your most Sincere Friend, G'l Wm. A. Bowles, D'r. Affairs, C.N." The rank of "general" was created by himself.

He was careful to make it appear to the Creek chiefs that his visit to New Orleans was voluntary. But the Spanish soldiers had guarded him well after his defeat at St. Marks.

When he found that Carondelet was not interested in his proposal to unite the Indian tribes with Spain to resist American attempts to appropriate their lands, he offered his services to Spain. In a letter to Carondelet (March 14, 1792) he said: "I have already informed your Excellency that I have come to this Town, in order to do away all misunderstandings between the Creek Nation, and his Catholic Majesty's subjects in this country, in order to that and it is necessary that I should give your Excellency a more particular account of the state of Affairs in that country . . . The Creek Nation are the original inhabitants of all the Country called by Europeans East and West Florida, and extend as far north as the 36 degree of North Latitude, into what is called the state of Georgia. The Cherokees are the original inhabitants of all the country to the north as far as the Ohio. These nations have some time past united into one nation and formed a council consisting of their chiefs whose resolves guided the Affairs of the whole nation — and the Military force that was swayed by the dictates of this Council amount to 20,000 men."

He says further in his letter that the "United Nation" had formed an alliance with the Indians to the north as far as the "Lakes of Canada," and that "this wise policy" was "completed" by him to put an end to the cruel practice of arming the Indians against one another.

He then assured Carondelet that the Creeks considered "his Majesty" as a natural ally, and that he could improve the connection. For this purpose he offered his services to Spain, and promised to establish a secure barrier between the United States and Spanish territory.

Carondelet did not, of course, believe any of this. He knew that Bowles was a plausible liar, and in every respect untrustworthy.

Since Carondelet did not have the authority to negotiate with Bowles he sent him under guard to General Las Casas at Havana, justifying his action on the ground that he had written the safe conduct before he learned of the capture of the store of Panton, Leslie & Company. This was, of course, a flimsy excuse, and certainly is a blot upon Carondelet's fame. Captain Don Pedro Rousseau reluctantly commanded the vessel which conveyed Bowles to Havana, although he himself had a high contempt for Bowles. The prisoner was held at Havana until Las Casas was informed of the "will of the King." The Spanish government finally ordered him sent to Madrid, where he remained until the authorities sent him to the Philippines for a long term in prison. But after serving nearly seven years he escaped to England, and there (he said) met William Pitt, England's prime minister, who encouraged him to return to Florida and continue his work. Anyway he was transported to Florida on a schooner of the Royal navy in September 1799, and upon his arrival proclaimed himself Director General of the Creeks.

He then entered upon his career as a pirate on the coast of Florida. He was a very formidable pirate whose schooners (he had several) were armed with ammunitions of war, and manned by Indians and worthless American and English sailors. He seized great stores of merchandise from merchant vessels on the Gulf of Mexico and on Lake Pontchartrain, especially those plying between New Orleans and Havana. In some cases he captured the vessel and placed it in his service. He thus acquired a good number of boats for his use. He made an attempt to capture the fort of Apalache, but Rousseau drove him off and captured one of his vessels.

Spain and the United States offered a reward for the capture of Bowles, and Rousseau was commissioned to take him at any cost, for he was a skilful operator and no merchant vessel was safe as long as he roved the seas. In one raid he captured as many as 900 barrels of flour enroute to Havana from New Orleans.

Having heard of the reward, some Indians captured him and tied him up with a rope while waiting for Rousseau's fleet to arrive and take him. But he gnawed the rope in the night while the Indians were asleep and escaped.

Captain Don Pedro Rousseau pursued him, and the

account of the exciting chase that followed was related by John Alfred Rousseau, the Captain's great-great-grandson, who has an accurate record of the manner in which Bowles was captured.

Bowles was eminently capable. Had he used his talents properly he could have risen to fame. That is what Pierre George Rousseau said of him. But he was a menace to the Spanish colonies in America and also to the United States.

After capturing the schooner Betsy, which belonged to Bowles, and burning one of his schooners, Rousseau followed him to Apalachee but lost track of him. He had gone to the chief of the Miccosukees, Kinhaizee, who sheltered him for a while but growing tired of his conduct decided to deliver him (for a price) to the commandant at Apalachee, and went to headquarters there for the purpose. But the commandant's wife took offense at the smell of the chief's pipe, and he promptly left, without a word of explanation, and turned his warriors over to Bowles.

A few days later Bowles' army, composed mainly of Indians, captured this Spanish fort (St. Marks near Apalachee) on May 20, 1800. But Rousseau with a fleet of seven men-of-war set out from Pensacola to Apalachee Bay, and one of his vessels sailed up the river and began bombarding the place. Bowles and his men fled.

The Miccosukees sheltered Bowles for about two years longer, and during this time he continued to lead expeditions to plunder and rob. But Rousseau pursued him, and, after a desperate fight lasting two hours, defeated his small army, and took him to Morro Castle in chains. There are conflicting reports concerning where this capture took place. But a traditional account reported by John Alfred Rousseau, a great-great-grandson of Captain Rousseau, avers that Bowles was captured in Natchez. He has in his possession a figure of Bowles' head sculptured in silver, which was taken from the handle of his sword.

While Bowles was lodged in prison the governor of Cuba sent him word that he would visit him. But Bowles sent him this reply: "I am fallen low but not so low as to receive a visit from the governor of Cuba."

He died in Morro Castle on December 23, 1805, and that was the end of an able man who, had he used his talents wisely, could have been of great value to his native land or to any country he wished to adopt.

Panton, Leslie and Company

After the Boston Tea Party many Tory citizens and merchants moved to Florida from the Thirteen Colonies, and among them was the great trading firm of Panton, Leslie & Company of Charleston, South Carolina. This firm, headed by William Panton and John Forbes, first moved to St. Augustine but later found Pensacola better suited to its trade and moved its headquarters there, maintaining the post at St. Augustine as a branch, and establishing also branches at St. Marks, Apalachicola, Mobile, Chicasaw Bluff and other small inland villages. Its trade was extensive and its profits were great, running into the millions of dollars. Long lines of pack horses went out into the interior, even as far north as the Tennessee River, carrying goods to the Indians and settlers of the country and bringing back skins, furs, honey, beeswax, jerked venison, and many other products for export and also for sale locally. Florida was then (1763-1781) held by the British.

When Spain captured Pensacola from the British in 1781 and took possession of Florida, the terms of surrender were very severe on the English inhabitants; it was decreed that they could remain in the province but all who did so must accept the Catholic faith. Those who refused to do this were allowed twenty-two months to dispose of their property. The majority of them left, and were compelled to sell their property for whatever they could get, which was not much, for buyers were eager to take advantage of the situation in which the sellers were placed. But a notable exception to this rule was the firm of Panton, Leslie & Company. This firm was not only permitted to remain on its own terms but was granted a commercial monopoly as an inducement to retain its trading posts throughout the territory. William Panton and his associates were not required to change their religious affiliations. They were granted all the privileges of the high-ranking officials of the province, and their influence extended throughout Spanish America. This firm continued to live well into the nineteenth century but the progress of commerce with its improved facilities finally left it as an interesting historic landmark.

Carondelet Leaves Louisiana

The Spanish government in the autumn of 1797 appointed Carondelet to a command in Quito, and he left New Orleans for this post. Under his administration the city had progressed rapidly. Many municipal projects had been completed. A great number of merchants of Philadelphia and New York had established branches here, and Americans from all parts of the United States moved in with their families to settle. Many French royalists flying from the new French Republic, and most acceptable as citizens, made their home here, among them the Baron de Bastrop, the Marquis de Maison Rouge, M. de Lassus de St. Vrain, and others of French nobility.

Carondelet had not been without problems which taxed his energy. The Western people and a society of French Republicans of Philadelphia had threatened to invade Louisiana, and attempted to persuade the people of the colony to join them. He found it necessary to order Rousseau to prepare for the defence of Louisiana. He had handled this matter with considerable wisdom and left the colony in good order. He had made many friends in New Orleans and the people in general hated to see him depart from their midst.

Manuel Gayoso de Lemos Appointed Governor of Louisiana

Manuel Gayoso de Lemos was educated in England and "brought up at the Court of London." He entered the Spanish army and attained the rank of brigadier-general. His first assignment in the colony was commandant at Natchez, and he was appointed one of the commissioners of Spain to fix the boundary between Florida and the United States, Andrew Ellicot being the commissioner for the United States. He was a perfect master of the English language, and while stationed at Natchez married Miss Elizabeth Watts, daughter of one of the Anglo-American pioneers of Mississippi. Shortly after his marriage he built the famous house known as

CONCORD on his plantation two miles below Natchez. Much of the material in this mansion was brought directly from Spain. The mansion, for many years a showplace, was destroyed by fire in 1900. The town of Natchez (the settlement having been founded in 1716 by Bienville as Fort Rosalie) was laid out under his direction, and various improvements were made from time to time under his personal supervision.

In 1797 he succeeded Carondelet as governor of Louisiana. While governor he was engaged in a bitter conflict with the Intendant, Don Juan Ventura Morales, which ended only with his death in 1799 at the age of 48. He was of a convivial disposition, and his death was attributed to dissipation. A man of his period (Lieutenant Pope) who knew him well, said that he was of "majestic deportment, softened by manners the most engaging and polite." He died poor, a circumstance which would indicate that he was not directly or indirectly interested in trade speculations, as most of the other Spanish officers high and low of Louisiana were.

In the intrigue to separate the western states from the Union he acted as the representative of the Spanish governor (Carondelet). He and Rousseau were good friends, and they went together to New Madrid and the mouth of the Ohio River to erect a fort. The spot where the fort was built is now known as Bird's Point.

Gayoso was a devout Catholic and narrow in his religious views. He strenuously objected to the introduction of the Protestant religion in the colony. "The privilege of enjoying liberty of conscience is not extended beyond the first generation," he said in his ordinance, "but the children of those who enjoy it must positively be Catholics. Those who will not conform to this rule are not to be admitted, but are to be sent back out of the province immediately, even though they possess much property." And "in the Illinois," (at that time the country on both sides of the Mississippi was known as Illinois) "none shall be admitted but Catholics of the class of farmers and artisans."

This ordinance was issued in September of 1797. At that time a large number of Protestants had already settled in the province. The Spanish commandants, feeling that Gayoso was unwise in his regulation, and being anxious to have American settlers, permitted Protestants to establish themselves, after vague, general and perfunctory examination of the subject of their faith.

CONCORD, THE MANSION ON GAYOSO DE LEMOS' PLANTATION, ABOUT TWO MILES FROM NATCHEZ.
(It was destroyed by fire in 1900)

Manuel Gayoso de Lemos was first married to a beautiful Portuguese Princess, Theresa de Hopman, who died at CONCORD. He later married Eliza Watts, daughter of Stephen Watts and Frances Ashton. She died three months after their marriage, and he later married her younger sister, Margaret Cyrilla Watts. Gayoso's residence while governor of Louisiana was what is now the little Theatre at the corner of Chartres and St. Peter Streets. (See page 139)

Rousseau Active in The New Madrid Area During The Administration of Gayoso

During the period in which Gayoso was governor of Louisiana, Rousseau was very active in the vicinity of New Madrid, for the Western people (i.e., the people of the Ohio Valley) were demanding free access to the Mississippi down to the Gulf. This Spain had permitted by a treaty in 1795, recognizing the Mississippi as the western boundary of the United States for a period of three years. The term of the treaty had elapsed, and it was not renewed. The Spanish governor of Louisiana promptly prohibited the western inhabitants from using New Orleans as a place of deposit and export of goods. This aroused the Western people to indignation. "The Mississippi River is ours," they declared, "by the law of nature. Our rivers swell its volume and flow with it to the Gulf of Mexico." They demanded that the Congress of the United States take the necessary steps to protect what they considered their rights, and avowed that they would otherwise take measures "which our safety requires." Their slogan was "No protection, no allegiance."

Rousseau was commissioned by Gayoso to command the posts of New Madrid, Placaminas, and La Balisa, and he moved into that territory with his squadron of galleys well armed and ready for action. He wished fervently to avert bloodshed but was quite determined to protect Louisiana against the threatened invasion by the people of the Ohio Valley. He made a great effort to maintain peace, and succeeded, for no battle was ever fought. The United States reopened negotiations with Spain and the matter of navigation on the Mississippi was eventually settled, but not completely until the Louisiana Purchase was arranged.

Rousseau returned to New Orleans and was saddened by the sudden death of Governor Manuel Gayoso de Lemos, which occurred on July 25, 1799. He and Rousseau had been friends for many years.

Abandons New Madrid

Rousseau did not return to New Madrid or the country of the Upper Mississippi and the Ohio Valley. He felt that he had completed his work in this territory, for there was not to be any organized warfare for which he had made preparations. There were only raids, pillagings, and minor invasions by Indians and murderous gangs of thieves to quell. He was a naval officer and preferred to give battle to the enemy in the accepted manner of warfare on the seas, not to supervise the policing of a scattered population composed of a wide variety of aristocrats roughing it, merchants, traders, Indians both vicious and friendly, and the most daring, unscrupulous adventurers from the United States and Canada. The commandants of the various posts in this territory had ample facilities for dealing with the Indians and ruffians so far as possible, for Rousseau had left them well supplied with arms and ammunition. At that time the commandant at New Madrid was Don Enrique Peyroux, and Don Luis Lorimer was commandant at Cape Girardeau. These men were very capable.

Rousseau remained in New Orleans for a long period awaiting orders. His preference was to move his fleet to the Gulf coast where the maritime trade needed protection, for the seas were infested with formidable pirates.

As Lawrence Kinnaird says in "Spain in the Mississippi Valley," "In planning the defense of Louisiana against an attack by way of the Ohio and Mississippi, Carondelet relied heavily upon armed river boats. Armed crafts were placed under the command of Captain Pedro Rousseau, an experienced officer who had fought with Galvez at Pensacola during the Revolutionary War and had subsequently served on the Florida coast patrol at the time of the Bowles affair. When Carondelet received reports that Americans were forming a settlement below the Ohio, he sent Rousseau in the galiot La Fleche to make a reconnaissance. The captain set out from Natchez on January 5, and proceeded all the way to New Madrid but found no Americans. He .remained there from March 6 to March 19, inspected the fort and vicinity, and then returned to Natchez. In the following fall, rumors of the French invasion by way of the Ohio caused the governor to order a vigilant watch for hostile crafts on the Mississippi. In October, the mission of patrolling between Nogales and the mouth of the Arkansas was assigned to La Activa while La Fleche guarded the river from the Arkansas to the Ohio. Soon thereafter, three more galleys and one armed boat of a smaller class were put into service on the river and Rousseau established his headquarters at New Madrid. The only immediate result of these preparations was the arrest, in February 1794, of a Frenchman named Jean Pierre Pisgignoux as he was descending the Mis-

Casa Calvo Appointed Governor

At the death of Gayoso, Don Francisco Bouligny, a colonel of the regiment of Louisiana, became acting governor of Louisiana until Casa Calvo was formally appointed by the Spanish government. Calvo (whose name was Sebastian Calvo de la Puerta) had an interesting career aside from his sojourn in Louisiana. He was a brother of Pedro, the first count of Buena Vista, and by a royal dispatch of May 20, 1786, a Castilian title was granted him and he accordingly became Marquis of Casa Calvo. He had at the age of 18 accompanied O'Reilly to Louisiana. He served many years in the army, and was in command of the Island of San Domingo when that island was threatened with insurrection. From there he returned to Cuba, which was his native country. He was born at Havana. His term as governor of Louisiana was short (1799-1801) but he remained in Louisiana, and was one of the Spanish commissioners who delivered the keys of New Orleans to Laussat, the French Intendant of Louisiana on November 30, 1803, for the French Republic. On December 17, 1803, the Louisiana Purchase was announced.

After the Louisiana Purchase he was appointed commissioner of boundaries by the Spanish government but the United States suspected him of fomenting dissatisfaction among the people, and Governor Claiborne requested him to leave New Orleans. He went to Pensacola, and from there to Madrid, Spain, where his relative and friend, Gonsalo O'Ferrile, who was minister of war, persuaded him to join the party of Joseph Bonaparte, who had been made king of Spain by Napoleon, and as a reward he was appointed Lieutenant-General. During the reign of Joseph Bonaparte he held several important positions but at the end of

---

sissippi. The prisoner was taken to Nogales, interrogated, and later sent to New Orleans. In his attempt to prove that he was not a French agent, he gave much information about Clark and his associates and named many prominent inhabitants of Louisiana as participants in the conspiracy. However, a later report received by Carondelet from Michel Lacassagne, one of his Kentucky informants, concerning the conduct of Pisgignoux in the United States, indicated that in all probability he was involved in the Clark-Genet affair."

1813, when France was driven from the peninsula, he was forced to flee to Paris. He died there in May of 1820, after living for six years on remittances sent him from Cuba by his daughters, Catalina and Marie Antonia, as all his possessions had been embargoed. His property was restored after his death to his son, Pedro, who had become Colonel of the Militia of Cuba. This son, owing to his "unbalanced conduct," incurred the displeasure of the Captain-General of Cuba, Miguel Tacon, and was exiled to Madrid, where he died in 1837. The family title was carried on through the younger of his two daughters. The Counts of Buena Vista had the exclusive privilege of maintaining an abbatoir in Havana. This right was from a grant made to O'Reilly and transferred to the Marquis of Casa Calvo.

Salcedo Appointed Governor

Don Juan Manuel de Salcedo, a brigadier-general in the armies of Spain, arrived in Louisiana to succeed Casa Calvo as governor. He was immediately unfriendly to the United States, and especially to the Western people. One of his first measures was to send arms and equipment to Natchitoches with instructions that the militia there keep Americans out of the district. At the same time he issued a decree forbidding the granting of any land to a citizen of the United States. He also suspended the right of deposit at New Orleans by the Western people, which, of course, enraged them.

Rousseau had long been well established in the colony, having served for 23 years as commanding general of the galleys, and since Salcedo ignored him he felt free to carry on his work more or less as he pleased. He therefore moved his fleet into the Gulf of Mexico and operated in the vicinity of Apalache and the Sabine Islands, where he was busy capturing pirate vessels which were harassing coastwise and overseas shipping. He was opposed to molesting the shipping trade of the Western people on the Mississippi, and looked with disfavor upon Salcedo's order to keep Americans out of the Natchitoches district. There may have been some of his relatives among those who wished to settle there, for many Rousseau families migrated from South Carolina and Virginia to Florida, Louisiana, and Mississippi around that time. But irrespective of this he was not inclined to take part in Salcedo's plan, for he considered him, as most people did, a narrow, autocratic individual who governed with little wisdom. There was no sound reason for any of his proclamations and restrictions. There is no record of any correspondence or conversation between Salcedo and Rousseau, except when Rousseau went to Salcedo's home on October 17, 1801, to inform him of the mutiny of the Voltaire, and to advise him that he had placed the matter in the hands of Don Jacobo Dubreuil. He then returned to his fleet, no doubt disheartened by the turn of events, remembering his pleasant associations with the former governors of Louisiana.

Salcedo did not entirely ignore Rousseau, for he assigned him a commission at Pensacola and he proceeded to this port on the galley's flagship, which he commanded. For this purpose Salcedo gave him a passport.

The Passport:

Don Manuel de Salcedo, Colonel of the Royal Armies, Political and Military Governor of the Provinces of Louisiana and West Florida, Inspector of the Veteran Troops and Militia of the said Provinces, Royal Vice-Patron, Subdeligate Judge of the General Superintendent of Mails, etc.

Whereas, Lieutenant Colonel Don Pedro Rousseau, Commander of the Galleys Fleet of the Mississippi is now employed on a commission of the Service which I have given to his care, I hereby grant him free and safe passport, so that, with the Royal Schooner "The Catalina" of his command, and with the crew mentioned in the list which he carries with himself, he may go to the stronghold of Pensacola. I order the subjects of this government, and ask and request those who are not, to put no obstacles in his way. Given in New Orleans, on the 27th day of November, 1801.

Salcedo

Andres Lopez Armesto

NOTE:
The mutiny of the Voltaire is one of the strangest incidents in Louisiana history. The trial lasted a long time, and yet no newspaper published any account of it. There were about sixteen men implicated but there is no evidence anywhere of what happened to them. They were most likely pardoned, for Rousseau in all fairness took their part. He understood Langlois, and knew that he was a mean, contemptible officer. No doubt there are many descendants of these mutineers living in New Orleans today but they have never heard of the Voltaire. Yet we have Rousseau's signature on a letter asserting that this incident did take place.

The Mutiny of the Voltaire

When in August of 1801 the crew of the Voltaire, a Spanish vessel commanded by Francisco Langlois, mutinied at Sabine Island, six sailors, and a British boy, went to Don Pedro George Rousseau and said that they had deserted with the other members of the crew who mutinied. They themselves had not taken part in the mutiny. He listened to the story with interest and sympathy. But when they had finished he advised them that since Langlois was related to him he preferred to have the matter investigated by Jacobo Dubreuil, a lieutenant colonel in the Royal Army, stationed at San Marcos Apalachie. His reason for doing this was that the sailors had accused Langlois of using them roughly "as if they were slaves," and he wanted Dubreuil to make the investigation so that it could be made without any semblance of prejudice. He would then send the full report of what Dubreuil found to the king of Spain. The report which Dubreuil made to Rousseau concerning this incident covers 365 typewritten pages, and a copy of it is in the Library of Congress. General Archives of

Indies — File No. 169   Cuban Papers — 1801

The following is from papers in Spanish furnished by the Library of Congress and translated by Marco A. Almazan especially for this book.

Rousseau's letter to Dubreuil

At this moment there have appeared before me six sailors from the crew of the Galleys under my command, and an English boy, all of whom formed part of the crew of the Galley "Voltaire," which was privateering in search of three English boats that were causing harm to the Royal interests of His Majesty in the vicinity of the Sabine Islands and the Anclote Keys. The same sailors and the English boy claim to have deserted the aforementioned Galley on the 18th of this month, because the crew mutinied on the 18th against their Commander, the Lieutenant of Militia and Second Lieutenant of the Army, Don Francisco Langlois.

As this officer is a relative of mine, it does not seem proper to me that I should handle this case. Therefore, I am sending the six sailors and the English boy to you, in order that they may declare in your presence what were the circumstances that motivated this happening. I have accordingly issued orders that all men under my command whom you may need should be punctually at your service.

God be with you many years. — Aboard H. M. Galley Santa Catalina, at anchor in front of San Marcos de Apalache, on August 20, 1801.

Pedro Rousseau (Signature)

To Don Jacobo Dubreuil

Although Dubreuil made the report, Rousseau conveyed the mutineers to New Orleans, and delivered them to the proper authorities for trial, but when he did this he had nothing more to do with the matter. It is shown, however, in the following pages that Rousseau did not have a very good opinion of his relative, Don Francisco Langlois, who evidently came of the Langlois family of Canada which had been prominent in that country, especially in military affairs, almost since its beginning.

THE TRIAL

In the City of New Orleans, on October 17, 1801, Don Manuel Garcia, Prosecutor in this trial, went with me, the Actuary, to the home of the Governor General of these provinces, Colonel Don Manuel Juan Salcedo, whereupon the Lieutenant Colonel Don Pedro Rousseau appeared before the said Prosecutor, who made him extend his right hand over the hilt of his sword and

Asked if he promised upon his word of honor to

answer the truth about what he knows and should be questioned.

He answered yes, I promise.

Asked what his name and occupation were.

He answered his name was Don Pedro Rousseau and that he is a Lieutenant Colonel of the Royal Armies, that he is Commander of the Galley Fleet and of the Galley "Santa Catalina" in the name of His Majesty.

Asked if he had been in charge of bringing some prisoners aboard the boat of his command, in which case he was requested to tell by whom and where the said prisoners had been delivered to him, what the names of the prisoners were and if they took refuge in any church while they were under his care.

He answered he had brought twelve prisoners who had been delivered to him by Don Jacobo Dubreuil, Commander of the Fort of Apalache. That when arriving in this capital he had delivered the prisoners, by order of the Governor, to his assistant the Lieutenant of the Regiment of Louisiana Don Josef Cruzat on the 27th day of Last month; that the prisoners were named Jose Reus, Jose Badia, Jose Valet, Jose Estrada, Jose Ramires, Jose Maria Escobar, Jose Maria Garcia, Jose de Mier, Miguel Mena, also known as Rodrigues, Augustin Flores, Francisco Sanchez and Antonio Martinez; that no one took refuge in any church while they were under his care; that he has nothing else to say; that what he has said is the truth, upon the word of honor he gave, all of which he had confirmed and affirmed when this deposition was read to him. He said to be of fifty years of age and signed this deposition together with the aforementioned Prosecutors and this Actuary. Manuel Garcia (Signature) — Pedro Rousseau. — Before me, Jose Betancourt. (Signature).

THE MUTINEERS TELL THEIR STORY

On August 20, 1801, six Spanish sailors and an English boy by the name of Thomas Forlong presented themselves to Don Pedro Rousseau, Commander of the Galley Fleet of the Mississippi, then at anchor in Apalache, to inform him that they had deserted the

schooner "Voltaire" because part of its crew had mutinied against their commander, Lieutenant Francisco
Langlois.

Rousseau decided it would be better for him not to
handle the case, since Langlois was a relative of his
and this was not the first time he had been in trouble
with men under his command. Therefore, he sent the
seven deserters directly to the commander of the fort
of San Marcos de Apalache, Lieutenant Colonel Jacobo
Dubreuil, with instructions to take care of the case.

Dubreuil took immediate action. He named the
soldier Jose Almogabar as Actuary and proceeded on
the same day to take the depositions of the deserters,
who were more dead than alive after three days and
three nights of continuous rowing in a small boat, without water or food, fleeing from the rebellious schooner
which had chased them almost to the entrance of Apalache Bay.

Only five of them had been interrogated, however,
when late in the same afternoon the "Voltaire" itself
was described near the shoals guarding the mouth of
the bay. Dubreuil ordered a canoe to approach the
schooner cautiously, while he made ready to pursue
and attack the mutinous vessel if need should arise. But
soon afterwards the canoe returned to the Fort with
two wounded men aboard: Commander Langlois and
the boatswain Francisco Silva — this latter in a state
of coma. The canoe also brought news of a peaceful
crew, who were only waiting for the tide to rise in
order to enter the bay.

About ten o'clock the next morning, after having
spent the previous night in the vicinity of the shoals,
the schooner sailed in and moored at the Fort, instead
of having set sail to the high seas as nearly everyone in
Apalache had expected her to do. Much to the admira-
tion of the Fort authorities, the mutineers proceeded
to disembark, and calmly presented themselves to Rousseau, who found them to be (as he had expected), a
group of frightened poor devils instead of the blood-
thirsty tigers Langlois had described the night before.

Rousseau knew well both his relative and his men,

and since the arrival of the deserters his intuition had told him that Langlois must have borne a sizeable share of the blame for the happening on board the "Voltaire." This was not the first time the hot-tempered Lieutenant had caused the men under his command to revolt against his cruel treatment and harshness. By the same token, Rousseau knew the men of his galleys were not intrinsically bad, and he was positive that after the flare of their revolt they would be so frightened by their action they would peacefully surrender themselves. He was so sure that he ignored Langlois' pressing entreaties to attack the schooner while it was at the shoals, as well as Dubreuil's suggestion to capture the mutinous crew before they put out to sea. Rousseau refused to take action and decided to wait for the men of the "Voltaire" to give themselves up. And so they did, on the morning of the 21st.

Again, Dubreuil was put in care of the situation. He finished cross-examining the deserters and proceeded immediately to take the depositions of Langlois and some of the men who, although not having taken part in the mutiny, had remained on board the "Voltaire" until it arrived at Apalache.

From these depositions Dubreuil gathered the case was more serious than it had seemed at first, and realizing that Lieutenant Langlois was greatly responsible for the happenings on the schooner, decided not to try the mutineers but to send them to the higher authorities in New Orleans. Therefore, on the 23rd he suspended the proceedings and placed all the men concerned under the care of Rousseau, who was to convey them to the capital of the colony.

There were only two casualties of the mutiny, Lieutenant Langlois and the boatswain Francisco Silva. The condition of the former was not serious at all. He had been wounded by a rifle bullet in the upper part of the right arm and by a cannon ball of small caliber in the back and in the lower part of the abdomen. According to surgeon Pedro de la Puente, who examined them while still in Apalache, "the healing of Langlois' wounds would be a matter of a short time." The boastwain Silva, on the contrary, was seriously injured as a result of a wound by rifle bullet in the head between the right eyebrow and the temple. Silva developed a high fever which kept him unconscious most of the time, until he finally died in the Fort on the night of the 26th.

Two days later Rousseau placed as prisoners on board his flagship "Catalina" the twelve men who had taken active part in the mutiny. These were: the gunner Jose Reus, who had led the revolt, the sailor Jose Badia, Jose Valet, Jose Estrada, Jose Ramires, Jose de Mier, Miguel Mena, Augustin Flores, Francisco Sanchez, Antonio Martinez, the mulatto Jose Maria Garcia and the negro Jose Maria Escobar.

Rousseau waited for good weather and sailed from Apalache on September 8, arriving in New Orleans nineteen days later. The fleet anchored in Bayou St. John and Rousseau presented himself to Governor Salcedo, who ordered the mutineers to be confined to the "calaboza," under care of Lieutenant Jose Cruzat.

On October 13 Governor Salcedo named Captain Manuel Garcia as Prosecutor in the trial to take place, and six days later began the tedious and long-winded cross examinations of the men who had mutinied aboard the "Voltaire."

The File No. 169 of the Cuban Documents of the General Archives of Indies, from which this relation has been taken, ends abruptly in the middle of the deposition of the mutineer Jose Badia, on December 9, and therefore we do not know what was the fate of the mutineers nor how the whole case ended.

Yet, from the depositions of Langlois, the deserters, the sailors who did not take part in either event, and from those of some of the mutineers, all rendered in New Orleans from October 19 to December 9, 1801, we can gather that the events preceding and following the mutiny, as well as the mutiny itself, took place in the following manner:

On August 7, 1801, the Schooner "Voltaire," of the Royal Galley Fleet of the Mississippi, sailed from Apalache to the Sabine Islands and Anclote Keys in pursuit of three English boats which were supposed to be trading with the Indians of western Florida. The schooner was under the command of Lieutenant Francisco Langlois, a harsh, cruel man whose mere name was hated by the men of the Galley Fleet.

From the very first day of navigation trouble started between the commander and his crew. That afternoon, about six o'clock, the sailor Jose Valet went to the kitchen to make some coffee. Langlois, who had been drinking, saw him and flew into a rage, shouting at the sailor to take away the coffee pot, for there was no sense in wasting water in making coffee when they might be short of it for the trip. Valet obeyed without replying and, knowing the temper of the commander, made haste to leave the kitchen. Langlois, however, waited for him at the door and gave him a brutal stroke with a club he carried for disciplinary purposes.

That night before supper the boatswain Francisco Silva — who was to die at Apalache as a result of the wound received in the mutiny — went to the Second in Command Ignacio Sierra and suggested that he ask Langlois not to abuse the crew but to punish those who deserved it by placing them in irons at the spar, as the Regulations stated, instead of striking them with clubs. Sierra, who seems to have been loved by the crew and held in respect by Langlois, went to the commander and reminded him that the Regulations forbade striking the men aboard His Majesty's ships, suggesting that he be less harsh if he wished to keep the respect and appreciation of his crew. Langlois, drunk by this time, wailed for half an hour that he wanted discipline on board and that he intended to have it at any cost.

The "Voltaire" continued its course and eventually arrived at the Sabine Islands, where no English boats were found. Langlois ordered to proceed to the Anclote Keys, but a few days later the shallowness of the waters prevented the schooner from reaching her destination and it was decided to return to the Fort.

On the 15th the "Voltaire" now enroute to Apalache, arrived again at the Sabine Islands, and following the suggestion of the Second in Command Sierra, it was decided to take shelter in the isles to avoid the threatening bad weather.

The next day, August 16th, a few men went ashore

to cut wood, get water and fish and hunt. When they returned on board, the steward Jose Estrada gathered the fish they caught and began to clean it on deck. Shortly afterwards he went to the kitchen and, opening the box where the salted meat was kept, he took two handfuls of salt to use on the fish. Again Langlois flew into a rage. Spluttering in French and Spanish he came to the steward and ordered him not to waste salt on the fish. Estrada quietly put the salt back in the meat box, locked it and went away.

But Langlois was still furious. He followed the steward, shouting insults after him, until he encountered the boatswain Silva and took it up with him. The commander accused Silva of being too lax with the men, who by this time were so undisciplined that they would dare anything on board without asking the approval of their commander.

The Second in Command Sierra, attracted by the uproar, entreated Langlois to calm himself, pointing out that the steward Estrada, being responsible for the provisions on board, would pay for anything found missing or spoiled. Sierra proved the injustice of scolding the boatswain, who had had nothing to do with the incident.

Langlois muttered something in French and went away to the kitchen. There he found the second boatswain Antonio Martinez who, having seen that a pot on the stove was overflowing with fish, was throwing some slices of it into the sea. This proved fresh fuel for the commander's rage.

"What is your business in this kitchen?" he shouted, "Are you the cook, or what?"

Martinez replied that the cook was busy at the moment and that having noticed the pot was too full of fish he decided to remove some.

In reply the commander struck the boatswain in the face, knocking him into the hold, where the sailor Ortega caught him in his arms.

"You dirty pig!" roared Langlois. "You were throwing the fish into the sea, thinking you were throwing it into my face!!"

The Second Boatswain got to his feet and with

clenched fists told Langlois that was no way to treat a ship's officer, and that if he would strike him in front of the men, they would lose all respect for him.

Langlois seemingly verged on an attack of hysteria.

"I will see that everyone obeys me on this ship!" he cried, threatening Martinez with his club. "Get out out of here and don't let me see you again in this kitchen!"

The boatswain left in silence and the remainder of the afternoon passed quietly.

That night, after supper, several sailors gathered in the bow and began to sing and dance to the beat of a tambourine. There was, however, a certain tension in the air, and it was plain that the crew resented the behavior of their commander. Small groups of men talked in low voices, suddenly falling silent the moment an officer approached. Langlois, uneasy, decided to spend the night lying on the chest of arms at the stern.

About half past eight the sailor Miguel Mena, after talking in low voice with a small group of men, detached himself from the dancers at the bow and went aft. With a coat slung over his left shoulder and his right hand under the coat, as if he were hiding something, he slowly approached the dozing Langlois.

The commander awakened upon hearing footsteps and sat up on the chest of arms, looking at Mena with mixed fear and astonishment.

"I have come to you in the name of the crew," began the sailor, "to ask you not to be so harsh. We are Spaniards, not Negroes as those you have been accustomed to command, and therefore we expect better treatment. Don't take this as an insubordination. It is not intended to be."

"Have you ever seen me punish anyone who didn't deserve it?" said Langlois, looking around.

"Yes, I have. Many times. Only this afternoon, you struck the Second Boatswain for no reason at all," continued Mena, drawing closer to Langlois.

"I want discipline on this vessel," shouted Langlois, reaching for a cutlass in the darkness.

His shout awoke a few men who were sleeping nearby. Two or three got to their feet and came towards the chest of arms.

"Fire!" shouted Mena, leaping into the kitchen, "fire on those aft!"

The gun at the bow, which had been turned aft, was fired by Reus, amid the shouts of his group and the confused scrambling of those who had been sleeping on deck. Immediately afterwards a starboard gun fired too, setting off two others on the same side and raising a cloud of smoke.

The men astern jumped overboard into the sea, while the mutineers at the bow, armed with knives, cutlasses and old rifles, advanced toward the stern led by Jose Reus, the gunner, and the sailors Jose Valet and Jose Ramirez.

Their first action was to open the chest of arms, from which they took rifles and distributed them among themselves. Then they lit a lamp and went searching for Langlois in his cabin, until someone raised his voice above the din and shouted that the commander had jumped overboard and was in the water. The party ran to the rail and began to search the darkness with the lamp until they found Langlois, scared to death, hanging on to the rudder.

"There he is! Here he is!" cried Jose Valet. "At last, our time for revenge has come!"

Five rifles pointed at the head of the commander.

At that moment the Second In Command Sierra, who had also jumped overboard, came to the surface next to Langlois, to find the muzzles of the rifles over his head.

"Don't kill me!" he implored, "I have a wife and son! Have mercy!"

The men assured Sierra they did not intend to harm him, nor any other of the officers, and that all their grievances were against "that scoundrel of Langlois." The men helped Sierra to get on board while the sailor Jose Valet jumped into the small boat which had been lowered to the side of the schooner and went to Langlois, pointing a pistol at his head.

Once more the Second in Command intervened and persuaded the men not to kill the commander. Reluctantly, they brought him back on board, where the sailor Ramirez grabbed him by the collar and shook him furiously.

"Now we'll teach you to deal with Spaniards! You are going to find the difference between dealing with them and your Negroes from the end of a rope. Let us hang the scoundrel from the mainmast!"

Sierra, dripping water, made his way among the men and took Langlois by an arm.

"Boys!" he said, "you better watch what you are doing. Monsieur Langlois is an officer. If you hang him it won't be long until you are hung too! Don't kill him. Put him in the spar if you wish, but spare his life."

Martinez noticed the commander was wounded and suggested that they take him aft and leave him under guard until they decided what to do with him. The group took Langlois to the spar and two sailors cured his wounds with brandy.

Reus ordered all the crew to convene at the bow and when all the men were assembled asked them who did not like what had happened.

The frightened men did not answer.

"If there is anyone who doesn't like it, I will give him a *peseta!*" said Reus.

This *peseta* (Spanish unit of currency), was, as everyone knew, a coin of that denomination nailed to the hilt of a large knife the gunner had carried with him.

Reus waited a few moments and, having no answer, ordered the boatswain Martinez to sound silence, and the men to go to sleep. He put two men to guard Langlois and gathering the mutineers went to the chest of arms, where they deliberated in low voices.

Next day, the 17th, the mutineers drew up a paper, stating the behavior of Langlois and relating the events and the reasons for which they had rebelled. They gave the paper to Langlois to read and sign, which he did readily, and then to all the men aboard, who stamped their signatures and marks in the document after hearing that a "peseta" was being offered again to those who would not.

Reus conferred with the men to decide where to go

or what to do. Some of them suggested that they go to Providence, in the Bahamas, and place themselves under the protection of the English, but the pilot Renato Bluche pointed out that his navigation chart only reached Tampa Bay and that he was not able to sail the ship any farther. Someone else mentioned Havana and Jamaica, but both suggestions were discarded for the same reason of not having a proper chart. Reus was very much in favor of "finding their fortune at sea," and still another came out with the idea of going to New Orleans and seeking refuge in a church.

While the mutineers were occupied with these deliberations, the sailor Jose Novelo, who had not taken part in the mutiny, went to Reus and asked his permission to go ashore with a small party to get water and wood. Reus agreed and told him to select his men and take the small boat. Novelo asked then to take two rifles and an ax, to try to kill some birds for the wounded and to cut some wood. Again Reus agreed and Novelo gathered six men, lowered the boat and went ashore. Among the men he chose was the English boy Thomas Forlong, whom he decided to take along after having heard the Negro Jose Escobar say that if the English youth was an obstacle if they decided to go to Providence, they should take him by the feet and smash his head against a gun.

This English boy, who was 15 years old, was from Bermuda and had originally sailed from Providence on an English schooner to trade with the Indians of Apalache. His ship, however, had been captured in the vicinity of the Sabine Islands by Rousseau's galleys and part of the crew taken prisoner. Forlong had been left to the care' of Ignacio Sierra, Second in Command aboard the "Voltaire," who had taken the youth along with him in the expedition resulting in mutiny.

Once the party of seven men was ashore, Novelo asked his companions if they were willing to desert and go to Apalache to inform the authorities of the happenings aboard the schooner. They all readily agreed, with the exception of Thomas Forlong who was afraid of the Indians and wanted to go back to the "Voltaire." But the rest believed it would be better to risk an encounter with the savages than to be found aboard a mutinous vessel and be tried for a crime in which they had not taken part. Accordingly, at three o'clock in the afternoon they sailed around a small cape to be out of sight of the schooner and headed straight for Apalache.

Next day, the 18th, at four o'clock in the afternoon the deserters descried a sail about two leagues and a half away, which they took to be an English corsair. On the 19th they saw the sail again, and on the 20th they recognized it as the "Voltaire." Rowing as fast as they could, for the schooner seemed to be in pursuit, the seven men finally arrived at Apalache, where they presented themselves to Rousseau, Commander of the Galley Fleet.

In the meantime, the men aboard the schooner, seeing that the small boat and its occupants had not returned by sundown, fired a gun and lowered the flag as a sign of distress. The boat did not return, as we have seen, and the mutineers began to feel uneasy, as they were positive the deserters had gone to Apalache to contact the authorities.

The Second in Command, Ignacio Sierra, again had something to suggest in his endeavour to find an easy solution to the problems which had arisen. At the same time, he was trying desperately to save Langlois' life, as some of the mutineers were thinking again of the convenience of preparing a rope for the mainmast. Sierra presented to the consideration of the men a scheme by which a document should be drawn up, stating that the happenings on board the "Voltaire" had been merely the consequence of an unfortunate accident: a gun had been turned aft and a sailor had passed by near the fuse with a lit cigar, thus causing the gun to fire and to wound Langlois and Silva. This document, he added, was to be signed by Langlois, the officers, and all the men; Langlois was to reassume command of the schooner, the "Voltaire" was to try to arrive in Apalache before the group which had deserted in the small boat, and he, Sierra, was to explain everything to the satisfaction of the authorities at the Fort, with the help and support of Langlois.

111

Langlois seemingly approved heartily of the plan. He talked to the mutineers in eloquent terms, pledging his word of honor as an officer and a gentleman that he would observe faithfully the conditions stated in the document to be drawn up, and promised that he would be the first one to convince the authorities in Apalache that all had been an accident. What is more, he apologized to the men for his behavior and promised never to be harsh again. He blamed his past attitude on the "acursed drinking" and begged the crew to go back to Apalache, where he was sure everything would be straightened out.

His speech impressed the mutineers. Two or three were suspicious of Langlois' sincerity and insisted they should set out to sea and put as much water as possible between the schooner and Apalache, but the majority believed in the commander's word, and it was decided to sail to the Fort. Jose de Mier and Jose Estrada drew up a new document, which everyone signed — this was without any "peseta" being offered to those who would not. Reus ceased to command, and the "Voltaire" made ready to sail for the coast on the next morning, as the pilot did not want to venture among the islands at night.

On the morning of the 18th the schooner left the Sabines and sailed against an unfavorable wind. Next day its crew saw the small boat, but despite their efforts to approach it, they could not even come close to it, as the deserters were rowing close to the shore, where the water was too shallow for the "Voltaire." On the morning of the 20th the crew saw the small boat enter Apalache Bay, which was cause of great regret as they had wanted the deserters to subscribe to the new agreement and to sign the document. Otherwise, the authorities at Apalache would hear first the real version of the course of events, as we already know it actually happened.

However, before the schooner entered the bay, the Second in Command Sierra and the boatswain Martinez went to Langlois in the name of the crew and asked him if he still promised to do everything within his power to save the lives of the mutineers. The Commander protested loudly that they should doubt the word of a French officer and gentleman, and congregating the crew he made a new speech, reassuring them he would observe the document he signed and defend "everyone's life as if it were his own."

Again the mutineers were appeased. Believing in the words of their commander, they let go the last opportunity to escape and decided to spend the night in the vicinity of the shoals.

Late that afternoon a canoe came from the Fort, to take the wounded ashore. Langlois and Silva boarded it, the former shaking hands with members of his crew and telling them not to worry about anything, that the moment he landed he would straighten out the whole affair and that by the morrow they could land without concern.

The canoe left the schooner. Ignacio Sierra, the Second in Command, who had remained aboard the "Voltaire," as a precaution against a sudden change of mind, ran the schooner aground on a sand bank and spent the night by the helm.

Next morning, with the tide, the "Voltaire" sailed into the bay and moored in front of the Fort, where Rousseau was calmly awaiting the men.

What happened to Langlois and the mutineers? The record, as we said before, ends abruptly with the deposition of one of the mutineers. The custom of that day was to hang mutineers and throw their bodies into the river. But there is no available account at present of what actually happened to the twelve men or to Langlois. We are hopeful, however, that we can trace these men and find their story. Research for this purpose is now being conducted.

There is no clear record to show how Francois Langlois was related to Rousseau. A native of Kaskaskia, Illinois, he was a prominent character in New Madrid where, prior to his appointment as commander of the Voltaire, he commanded the Spanish galliot "Fleeche," the gunboat "Toro" and the batteau "Prince of the Austrias." He was generally hated by the men under his command. Regardless of his high rank in the Spanish navy he was not considered a very trustworthy person, for General Wilkinson charged him with having received a lot in New Orleans from Daniel Clark to swear falsely against him (Wilkinson). The only available evidence of a possible relationship between him and Rousseau is that a Thomas Rousseau of Saintonge, France, (the birth place of Pierre George Rousseau) had a daughter, Genevieve, who married Jean-Francois Langlois in 1692, and resided in Canada with her husband. Their descendants migrated to Kaskaskia. If this was the relationship to which Rousseau referred it was very distant.

The Langlois family were among the very first settlers of Quebec, Sebastian Langlois, an army physician with the rank of general, moved his family there in 1634, and acquired great wealth. His children married into the best families of Canada, and their descendants continued for many generations to rank among the most affluent and influential people of that country.

A Langlois of this family, however, married Louise Helene Wiltz, the sister of Margaret Wiltz, who was Pierre George Rousseau's mother-in-law. Francisco Langlois was the son of Louise Helene and Langlois, and therefore first cousin of Rousseau's wife, Catherine. This was undoubtedly the relationship to which he referred.

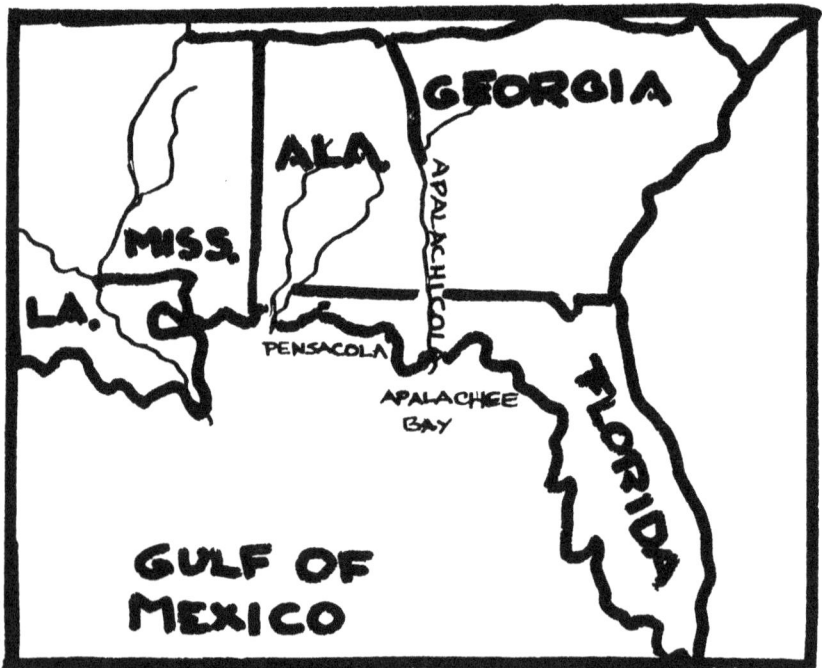

San Marcos de Apalache (the area shown on this map) is where Rousseau and Dubreuil on August 20, 1801, on H.M. Galley Santa Catalina, were stationed when they learned of the mutiny of the Voltaire.

Pierre George Rousseau Retires from The Spanish Service and Makes His Home in New Orleans

When Napoleon was at the head of the French government with the title of First Consul he persuaded the King of Spain to return Louisiana to France on condition that he made over to the Duke of Parma, who belonged to the royal house of Spain, that part of Italy known as the Duchy of Tuscany. This deal was consummated on October 1, 1800, and kept a profound secret. Spanish officials continued to administer the affairs of the colony. But Napoleon soon realized that as a maritime power England was superior to France, and she would most likely seize this colony when she learned of the transfer. He thus shrewdly sought and found an able and anxious purchaser in the United States. This was the third time this province called Louisiana was sold, transferred or returned from one nation to another without the knowledge of its people, quite as if it were a quantity of merchandise or a piece of real estate privately owned.

Now, since one of Spain's most important colonies, to which Don Pedro George Rousseau had given twenty-four years of honorable and efficient service, was sold to the United States, he would have to be transferred to some naval station in Spain or one of her other colonies if he remained an officer in the navy. He had married a native of New Orleans, and all his children were born there. This was his home and he did not wish to leave it. He had acted as commanding general of the galleys of the Mississippi (a post which gave him command not only of the fleet on the river but also on the Gulf of Mexico and the surrounding lakes) under all the seven Spanish governors of Louisiana from Galvez to Salcedo. His relations with each one had been very agreeable, and each had praised him highly for his ability and loyalty. He felt that considering the service he had rendered he was justified in requesting that he be retired at New Orleans on a pension.

His petition to the King of Spain, written by his attorney, clearly sets forth his record:

Petition for a Pension

(Notes from General Archives of the Indies, Seville — Papers from the Island of Cuba).

With documents of proof attached, the attorney who drew up the petition for a pension (his name is not given in the G.A.I. papers) clearly sets forth what he designated "THE SERVICES OF DON PEDRO ROUSSEAU, COMMANDANT OF THE GALLEYS OF THE MISSISSIPPI." He said that the Lieutenant-Colonel, by brevet, Don Pedro Rousseau, "declares before the royal feet of Your Majesty: that seeing with the greatest grief the sad moment for the surrender of this province to the Commissary of the French Republic, draw nigh, and after that to the United States of the North, in the critical condition of being in his advanced age surrounded by ten children who are just so many other obstacles to his ardent desire of consecrating his last days to Your Royal service, he finds no other refuge in his deplorable situation than that of applying to your sovereign kindness, always inexhaustible, towards the vassals who have enlisted under your royal banners, encouraged by the unequivocal proofs which he has given of his loyalty, zeal, and love for your august person, during the space of twenty-four years."

After this flattery and appeal for pity, which was then customary in asking the king a favor, the attorney listed Rousseau's accomplishments:

1. He reminded him that he had already been advised of Rousseau's distinguished conduct at the siege of Pensacola, and that his Secretary of State, Don Josef de Galvez, had written to give him thanks in his royal name.

2. Not less glorious was "the capture which he made on Lake Pontchartrain of the English sloop named 'West Florida', on boarding which he received two serious wounds."

3. That he had a part in "the conquest of Movila (Mobile), as commander of the above-mentioned Galveston."

4. That he "forced the Port of Pensacola, at the orders of Galvez, who was on his vessel. (The successful

result of his expeditions will be seen in documents Numbers 2, 3, and 4, attached)."

5. That by the above mentioned documents, and numbers 5 and 6, "Your Majesty will see that after he had served for two years in the post of Natchitoches to the satisfaction of your Governor, Don Esteban Miro, he succeeded in establishing himself with Colonel Don Manuel Gayoso de Lemos in the important post of Las Barrancas de Margot."

6. That "he put to flight the difficulties imposed by the Chicachas Indians, whose principal chief he induced to yield that territory to Your Majesty, as that chief really did so, after signing the suitable document of cession."

7. That, as can be seen from a certified copy of document No. 7, "having cooperated in the arrest of the adventurer, Guillermo Bowles . . . he took him to Havana."

8. That "from January 1792 to June 1796 he was employed in delicate and important commissions for your royal service, under the character of Commandant of the squadron of galleys."

9. That "in 1799 he captured the fort of San Marcos de Apalache, which had been conquered by the Indians; and in 1800, while commanding the schooner, Leal, . . . he captured two chaloupes, one being one of your ships, which had been captured by the English . . . He took six men prisoner. In the same year he captured the English schooner, Walther, armed with eight four-pounders which it was carrying as reinforcement to the adventurer, Bowles. In the year 1801, through well-given orders, he captured the Island of San Jorge (i.e. St. George) and Perro (i.e. Dog Island), the schooner named Fabarita, which was carrying ten cannons and ammunitions of war to the bandit, Bowles. A short time after this he captured the schooner, Betecy, (i.e., Betsy), owned by Don Jose Vidal, which had been captured by Bowles while sailing to Havana laden with 900 barrels of flour. After these events he . . . captured a hostile batteau laden with salt, and burnt a schooner belonging to Bowles."

10. That "he humbly entreats Your Majesty to deign to grant him his retirement in this city (i.e. Nueva Orleans) with the pay which may be your Royal pleasure, a grace which he hopes to receive from the sovereign charity of Your Majesty."

(Signed: Pedro Rousseau, at New Orleans,

November 15, 1803)

This is an odd document of more than 1200 words written to Charles IV of Spain. It is not, however, unlike those of a similar nature and for the same purpose (to procure retirement at New Orleans) written for Don Louis Lorimier, Antonio Soulard, and others. But they were not so elaborate as the one written for Rousseau. And yet if Rousseau signed this document it is doubtful that he read it carefully, for there are apparent errors in it. The documents attached as proof of his activities and achievements in his service to the colony were undoubtedly correct, for they were public records. But the references to his advanced age and his great need in view of the ten children dependent upon him for support are incorrect. He was neither old nor poor; he was fifty-two years old. But for the purpose of impressing the King this statement was permissible, for in those times a man of that age could easily be referred to as old. The vast plantation and slaves owned by his family on the river, composing the section which later became Lafayette City, were properties inherited by his wife. He owned nothing personally and had to depend upon his salary, which for a lieutenant-colonel was very small (480 pesos fuertes in the beginning but increased later). The Spanish officials in power accorded him many honors and gave him many responsibilities but did not pay him a large salary. They gave him a land grant of eleven hundred acres in north Louisiana and approximately ten thousand acres in Honduras, it is said, but it was all a wilderness at the time and worthless to him. These land grants were not listed in the inventory of his succession. But eighty years later his great-grandchildren claimed the land in

118

north Louisiana and sold it to divide the proceeds. Each received about five dollars.

The statement that he had ten children in 1803 is incorrect; he had seven. He later had five more, the last being born in 1808 when he was fifty-seven years old. Two of his sons entered the United States Navy as. midshipmen; the youngest, John Baptiste, was drowned while in service; Lawrence became one of the highest ranking officers in the United States Navy, and later served with distinction in the Confederate Navy. Octave S. became a judge in St. Bernard parish. Gustave Sebastian graduated from West Point and held the rank of Brigadier General, Louisiana Militia. He also led the Louisiana troops to the War with Mexico. Pierre Andre and Rodolphe were attorneys.

There is no available record as to whether Pierre George Rousseau received a pension from the Spanish government, for the Napoleonic war was raging and by 1808 Napoleon had forced Charles IV to abdicate in favor of his brother, Joseph Bonaparte.

Although Rousseau had won fame in the Spanish service he always spoke with pride of his service in the American Navy and of his appointment to the rank of captain by the Continental Congress, and so did his family. When Lafayette visited New Orleans in 1824 the newspaper stated that "In the early afternoon Lafayette made a tour of the City, and then visited Monsieur and Madame Bernard de Marigny and Mme. Rousseau, widow of Captain Rousseau, an officer of the Revolution."

Pierre George Rousseau died on August 8, 1810 at New Orleans. The newspapers of his day did not have the facilities, of course, of our modern publications, and apparently their reporters did not have the energy or interest of our present-day newsmen who gather facts with great care, and do not say "about so many children or he was about such and such an age" but take the trouble to ascertain the exact number. The reporters of the nineteenth century did not have the telephone. But the cities were small and they did not have far to walk. The COURIER gave his age as

119

59, which was correct, and stated that he had "eleven or twelve children." He had twelve. The GAZETTE stated that his age was 66. The COURIER'S statement was of course correct, for it agrees with the following baptismal record from the Archives de la Charente-Maritime:

REGISTRES PAROISSIAUX DE LA TREMBLADE
1750 - 1751

Le troisieme juin mille sept cent cinquante un est ne et ete Baptiste Pierre Georges fils legitime; de sieur Pierre Rousseaux capitaine de navires et Marie Eustelle Daniaud. Ont ete parein et mareine Georges et Henriette Rocher frere et soeur qui ont signe avec nous.

(signe) Rocher   la Rocher
Doussin, cure

The following is the account of the COURIER:

THE LOUISIANA COURIER
August 10, 1810

Died on Wednesday last on his plantation near this city, Mr. Peter Rousseau. European by birth, he came to this country almost an infant with his father, a Captain of merchant vessel. In the beginning of the war undertaken for the achievement of American Independence, he was employed in the Navy of the United States where he distinguished himself so eminently that he was elevated to the rank of Lieutenant of a frigate. He occupied this position until at the request of Mr. Galvez, Governor of Louisiana, he entered the service of Spain. Amongst the military expeditions in which he signalized himself may be reckoned those of La Mobile and Baton Rouge, and particularly that of Pensacola in which he acquired great glory by his intrepidity. He commanded the Spanish corvette Galveston who entered first into the harbor under the heavy fire of the English batteries. He was afterwards appointed Commanding General of the galleys of H C M, and decorated with the grade of Lieutenant Colonel. A good father, tender husband, good friend, and very commendable by his military capacity, Mr. Peter Rousseau carries with him the merited regrets of his spouse and eleven or twelve children, one of whom is in the service of the American Navy.

LOUISIANA GAZETTE, Thursday, August 9, 1810
Died — Yesterday at his plantation half a league above

the city Pierre Rousseau aged 66. He distinguished himself as a friend to the American Independence — was appointed by the Continental Congress a Captain in the Navy at the commencement of the Revolution and continued true and faithful to the cause until the close of the war. He was a kind benevolent husband and parent, a merciful and tender master.

(The COURIER was published in French and English. The account of his death in the French section states that he was 59, which was, of course, correct).

The following is a copy of the death certificate of Pierre George Rousseau (the original of which is in the hands of Mr. Robert G. Polack);

I, Friar Antonio de Sedella, Religious Capuchin, Rector of the Parochial Church of St. Louis of New Orleans, certify, in the way I can and as I should, that in one of the books of register of the deceased, which is the sixth in current issue, for white people only, on folio 433, there is a record of the death certificate, entered under number 784, and which reads as follows:

RECORD No. 784 Ninth day of August, of the year 1810, I, Friar Antonio de Sedella, Religious Capuchin, Rector of this Parochial Church of St. Louis of New Orleans, gave burial in the cemetery of said church to the remains of Don Pedro Jorge Rousseau, Lieutenant Colonel, retired and graduated from the the Army and pensioner in the service of his Catholic Majesty, a resident of this city, of about 60 years of age, born in Tremblade, the province of St. Onge, France, a legitimate son of Don Pedro Rousseau and Dona Maria Danivau (Daniaud), married to Dona Maria Margarita Milhet, deceased yesterday afternoon at two o'clock; and to make it known I sign this certificate.

Friar Antonio de Sedella

All the aforesaid agrees with the original record, which remains in the said book of register of the mentioned church; and having been asked to do so by a legitimate party, I issue this copy in New Orleans on January 21, 1811.

The Ancestry of Margaret Wiltz, Mother of Catherine Milhet Rousseau

Johan Theodor von Wilsz, a native of Eisenach, Thuringia, married Christine Francken. Two of their sons came to America. One settled in Mobile, Alabama.

The other, Johan Ludwig, born in 1711, settled in New Orleans. Before coming to Louisiana he married one of the Ziriac family of Saxony. After her death (in New Orleans) he married Marie Dolc, a native of Franckendel, Saxony. (It was Johan Ludwig who changed the name to Wiltz, dropping the title of Baron von Wilsz, although the family, it was said, had borne the title quite worthily). By this marriage to Dolc he had a daughter, Louise Helene, who married Francisco Langlois; another daughter, Margaret, who married (2) Jacinto Panis, and (1) Joseph Milhet.

Margaret and Joseph Milhet had two daughters. The younger daughter, Catherine, married Pierre George Rousseau. The older daughter, Margaret, married George Webre.

Margaret and George Webre had a daughter who married John Baptiste Ory; and a daughter, Euphemie, who married Auguste Gautier; their son, Samuel Edgar, married Alice Cassard, and their daughter, Ines, married Herbert C. Parker.

The brother of John Ludwig Wiltz, Joseph, married Suzzanne Zweig (or Suzzanne Labranche). Their son, Jean Laurent Wiltz, married Marianne Colomb.

Jean Laurent Wiltz and Marianne Colomb had a son, Jean Baptiste (whose portrait is in the Cabildo), He married (1) Suzzanne Langliche, and (2) Marie Josepha Bahy.

From Jean Baptiste's marriage to Langliche there was a son, Leonard (portrait in the Cabildo), who married Marie Piquery (portrait in the Cabildo). From this marriage Leonard had a daughter, Anne, who married her cousin, Edmond Valcour Wiltz, and a son, Everiste, who married Adelaide Montreuil.

From the marriage of Jean Baptiste to Marie Josepha Bahy, there was one son, Wisin, who married Louise Collier.

Louis Alfred Wiltz, who became Governor of Louisiana, was descended from Everiste Wiltz, who married Adelaide Montreuil.

The Rousseau Plantation

Pierre George Rousseau apparently had nothing more than his salary as an officer (1) in the American navy, which was undoubtedly small, and (2) in the Spanish service, which was also small. He could have acquired considerable wealth through land grants while he was in high favor with the Spanish authorities, as many Spanish officers did, with the notable exception of Manuel Gayoso de Lemos, his friend, a man of the highest probity, who did not use his office and influence for personal gain. Rousseau was dedicated to his profession, and money to him was a secondary matter.

But he had married into a family of considerable wealth, the evidence of which is in the following excerpt from "The History of the City of Lafayette," which appeared in the Louisiana Historical Quarterly, volume 1, of 1937:

Notes from "A History of The City of Lafayette" by Kathryn C. Briede

By 1810 the population of New Orleans had increased to such an extent that the various plantations immediately above the city had been divided into lots and made into faubourgs, as Faubourg Ste. Marie, Delord, L'Annunciation, etc. The population had spread out until settlers were to be found at the lower edge of the Nuns' plantation. The nuns, therefore, decided that the best way to dispose of their land was to have it laid out in lots which might be sold to new settlers. Sister Sainte Marie Olivier, the Superioress, together with Sister Sainte Felicite Alzas, her Assistant, and Sister Saint Andre Madiere, the Depositaire, held a conference with Messieurs F. V. Potier and Bartelmy Lafon, surveyors, in regard to the division and sale of this land.

On September 18, 1810 the surveyors submitted a plan dividing the tract into city lots. A road was to be run through the center of the tract from the river to the swamps in the rear. This road, later St. Mary Street, was evidently named Chemin de Ste. Marie in honor of the Mother Superior. In addition, two other roads were to be run parallel to this central road, and were to be called Chémin de St. Andre, later St. Andrew Street, and Chemin de Ste. Felicité, later Felicity Street, in honor of the Depositaire and Assistant, respectively.

The plan was accepted, and lots of land, usually measuring about three hundred feet in front, were sold. With the sale of this land and the consequent settlement of it, cross streets were constructed and buildings were erected. Thus came into being a new suburb of New Orleans, the Faubourg Nuns.

LAFAYETTE

The tract of land that later became known as Faubourg Lafayette existed for a long time as the *Wiltz tract*. This is perhaps due to the fact that in 1803 the title was confirmed by the United States Government in the name of *Marguerite Wiltz*. The extract from the AMERICAN STATE PAPERS reads as follows:

No. 142 — *Marguerite Wiltz* claims a tract of land situated in the county of Orleans, and on the left bank of the Mississippi, about one league above the city of New Orleans, containing four hundred and fifty superficial arpents, bounded on the upper side by land of James Livaudais, and on the lower by land claimed by the nuns of the city of New Orleans.

It appears to the Board, from a deed of conveyance, executed 28 March, 1758, before Jean Baptiste Carrie, notary public, that Augustus Chantaloux sold eight arpents of front, by a depth not defined of said land, to Stephen Vaugaine, which he alleges to have acquired as follows: six arpents, at the public sale made of the estate of one Dilmo, in 1752; and the other two arpents of front, by the depth aforesaid, of one Pidet, who had

---

*M. C. Soniat, "The Faubourgs Forming the Upper Section of the City of New Orleans. (Louisiana Historical Quarterly, xx 1837, 199.)

purchased the same from one Lagotre; and it also appearing to the Board, from a deed of conveyance likewise exhibited, that on the＿＿day of＿＿, 1769, the two arpents of front, by the depth aforesaid, (remainder of the quantity now claimed) was sold by the widow Laronde to James Livaudais; and it further appearing, from the deeds of conveyance exhibited, that the several tracts of land above described have been transferred to the present claimant, the Board do hereby confirm her said claim.

Marguerite Wiltz was the daughter of one Johan Ludwig Wiltz, of Eisenach, Thuringia, Saxony, by his second marriage to Marie Dohl, also of Saxony, in Louisiana. Soon after his first marriage to Miss Ziriac in Saxony in 1731, Mr. Wiltz and his wife came to New Orleans, and later became the owners of a farm at the Cote des Allemands on the Mississippi River. Marguerite was a very attractive and accomplished young woman, and, as such, attracted many suitors. From her wide choice of admirers, she chose and married Joseph Milhet, who was reputed at that time to be one of the richest French merchants in New Orleans. Milhet became involved in Nicolas Chauvin de Lafreniere's secret conspiracy in New Orleans and the neighboring parishes in 1768, to rid Louisiana of Spanish rule by driving the Spaniards from the colony. He was among those long remembered true patriots to be shot by order of the Spanish governor, General Alexander O'Reilly on October 25, 1769. Marguerite Wiltz Milhet was now a widow, left alone to care for her small daughter, Catherine.

In 1777, Marguerite married for the second time. Her new husband was Jacinto Panis, a Spanish Captain and Sergeant-Major in New Orleans. Several years later, Mr. Panis brought a parcel of land above New Orleans, which later formed a large part of the Faubourg Lafayette. This purchase comprised eight arpents of land which he bought from Mr. Etienne Vau-

American State Papers, Public Lands (Washington, 1834), 11, 313-314 S. C. Arthur and G. C. de Kernion, Old Families of Louisiana. Gayarre, op. cit. 11,343.

gine de Nieurman on August 2, 1779. The act of sale from which this date is derived traces back the ownership of this land, and thus one learns that until 1753 the land was owned by Louis Xavier Delino and his wife, Madelin Broutin, who sold it on September 12th of that year to Augustin Chantalou and his wife, Dame Marguerite Songy; it was sold on March 28, 1758, by these owners to Mr. Vaugine de Nieurman, who kept it until 1779.

Mr. Panis did not live very long, and by virtue of his last will and testament, dated August 24, 1786, drawn up by Fernando Rodrigues, his widow, Marguerite Wiltz Milhet Panis, became his sole and only heir. There were no children from this marriage.

The Wiltz tract contained ten arpents in all, eight of which have already been accounted for. The remaining two arpents were purchased by Mrs. Panis from her neighbor, Mr. Jacques Francois Livaudais, in the presence of Pierre Pedesclaux, Notary, on September 14, 1797. Mr. Livaudais had acquired this land from Widow Delaronde, together with much additional land in an act of sale passed before Jean Baptiste Garic in 1769.

Evidently, in 1806, Mrs. Panis conceived the idea of dividing the front portion of her land into lots and offering them for sale, because on January 10th of that year she had requested Barthelmy Lafon to have her entire plantation surveyed and to submit a plan of it to her. This plan must have been lost, because no record of it survives today.

By 1813, the property of the Ursuline nuns which had been surveyed and subdivided into lots was practically all sold, and the moving tide of population had reached the lower confines of the plantation of Widow Panis. Therefore, Mrs. Panis revived her idea of having her plantation divided, and, as a result of certain negotiations, Mr. F. V. Potier submitted a second prospectus to Mrs. Panis on May 23, 1813. The boundaries of

M. de Armas, Notarial Records (Jan.-June, 1818) This is from an act of sale numbered No. 379. Bis. and entitled "Vente D'habitation par Dame Milhet Rousseau au Sieur John Poultney."

the land which was divided into city lots were the Mississippi River, the Livaudais plantation, the middle of St. Andrew Street, and the middle of what was later known as Chippewa Street. The plan, which divided this section into one hundred lots, re-adjusted the Public Road or Levee Street (along the Mississippi River), and provided for a street to be called Rousseau Street, running parallel to the river. A street which was to be named "Cours Panis," was run through the center of the plantation, from the river to the rear of the tract; while above it were to be the two streets of Philippe and Soraparu; and below it, those of Josephine and Adele. "Cours Panis," now known as Jackson Avenue, owed its name to the owner herself, Widow Panis. Josephine and Philippe were probably named after the two children of the Saulet family, while Levee Street owed its appellation to the levee on its far side. Soraparu derived its title from Jean Baptiste Soraparu, an inhabitant of New Orleans, who was a close friend of the Panis family who often aided them in financial matters. Rousseau Street received its name from the Rousseau family, the son of which, Pierre George Rousseau, married Catherine Milhet.

As soon as the lots were put on the market, many were sold. The following citations will give some idea of the sale of these lots:

The lots designated on the plan by numbers 47, 54 and 55 to Mr. Lazare Pignatel according to act before Pierre Pedesclaux, Notary, dated May 26th, 1813.

Lots numbers 23, 24 and 35, as well as a portion having a forty foot front with a depth of twelve hundred feet, English measure and being next to the plantation of Mr. John Kilty Smith, according to another act before the same Pierre Pedesclaux, Notary, as of May 26, 1813.

Lots numbers 1, 2, 3, 4, 6, 7, 25 and 36 sold to Mr. Alexander Hamilton Smith, according to another act before the same Notary, Pierre Pedesclaux, dated July 10th, 1813.

Lots numbers 18, 19, 20, 21, and 33 to Mr. Patrick Wale, Junior, according to the act before the same Notary, Pierre Pedesclaux, bearing date of September 15, 1813; and lastly,

Lots numbers 44 and 76 and a portion forty feet wide by eighty feet in length, bounded on one side by Mr. Livaudais' property and on the other side by that of the Vendor, being a continuation of and next to that sold to Mr. Smith on May 6th, 1813, and to the same Mr. Smith according to another act before the same Notary, Pierre Pedesclaux, June 15th, 1815.

This seems to be the first appearance of English names in this vicinity. To the purchasers of these lots went the right of a free use of the batture, which Mrs. Panis had reserved for her own use. The right to take earth from the batture to be used in the construction of levees and roads, and the right to carry on commerce were also accorded to them. In case of repairs to the levees or an erection of a new one, the expense was to be borne by the owners of property and the Widow Panis, in proportion to the amount of land owned.

After the death of Mrs. Panis, the remaining unsold lots and the balance of the plantation became the property of her daughter, Catherine Milhet Rousseau, and was then known as the Rousseau plantation. On May 27, 1818, Mrs. Rousseau, now a widow, sold her holdings to Mr. John Poultney, a merchant from New Orleans, for the sum of $100,000. Of this amount $20,000 was to be paid in cash, and the remaining $80,000 was to be paid in five annual and equal payments of $16,000 each. It was agreed between the parties concerned, that if the purchaser could not pay any or all of the payments the property would become the possession of the persons who had signed the five annual notes, to the extent of the notes paid by them.

Almost one year after this purchase, Mr. Poultney found himself in embarrassed circumstances financially, so he applied to the District Court, on April 26, 1819, for a stay of proceedings and for permission to call a meeting of his creditors, with the view of obtaining an extension of credit. This meeting was accordingly ordered and held, and as a result, Mr. Poultney was given a respite of one, two, and three years for the payment of his debts. This was done because a schedule present-

M. de Armas, Notarial Records (Jan.-June 1818) This is written in French, and here is a free translation of part of it.

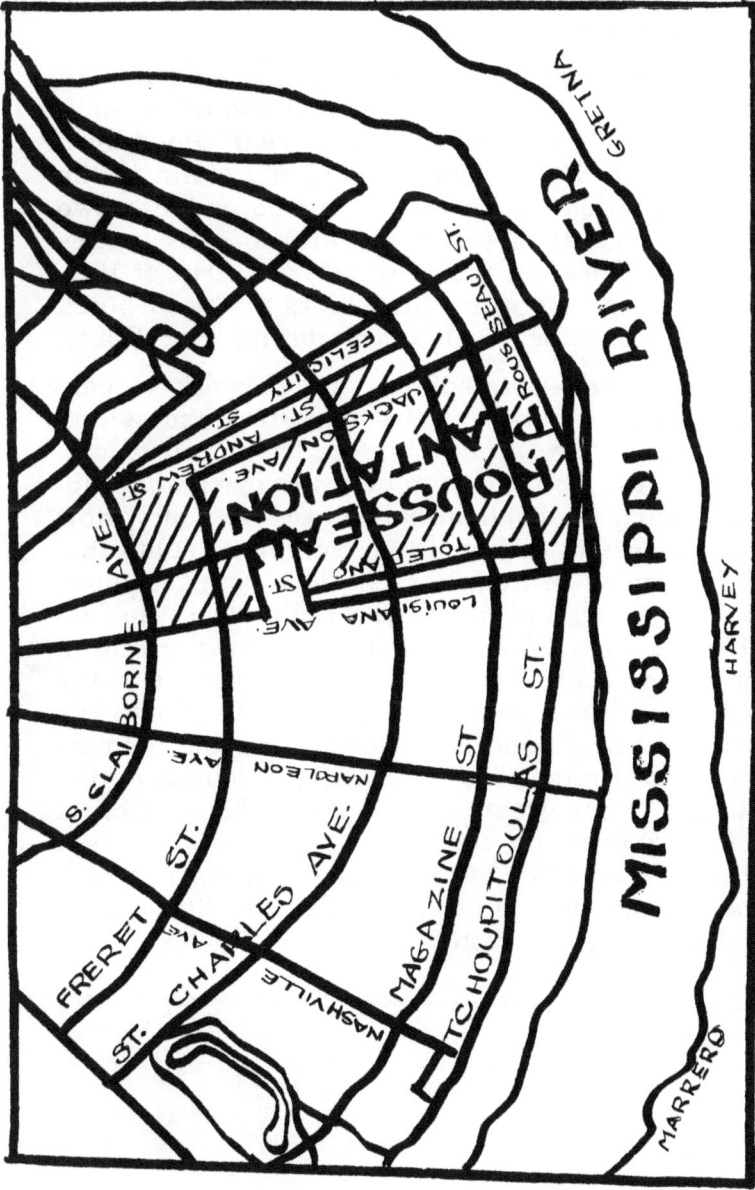

SKETCH-MAP OF PLANTATION

The Wiltz Tract (later known as the Rousseau Plantation) comprising 450 arpents, was located between Jackson Avenue and Louisiana Avenue. Margaret Wiltz Panis inherited this land, and formed a subdivision, naming the streets after members of her family. (Sketch furnished by John Alf. Rousseau)

ed by Mr. Poultney showed that his resources totaled $237,921, whereas his liabilities amounted only to $207,-295. Chief among Mr. Poultney's creditors were the firm of Harrod & Ogden, who paid the first note on the recently acquired property.

Mr. Poultney died on October 23, 1819, and left all his property and debts to his widow and two minor children. On January 26 of the following year, Poultney's widow made a formal renunciation of any claim to the Rousseau plantation on behalf of herself and her two minor daughters. As a result of various legal battles among the creditors, by the year 1824 the firm of Harrod & Ogden were the sole title-holders of the disputed property which once belonged to Marguerite Wiltz Panis.

The new owners immediately set to work to continue her plan of subdividing the plantation and selling more city lots. They accordingly called in surveyors, and had the rest of the plantation surveyed and subdivided following the original lines of the plan of Widow Panis. As a result, Joseph Pilie, Surveyor, submitted a plan to them on March 2, 1829. Two changes, however, took place at this time. The main street had its name changed from "Cours Panis" to Jackson Street in honor of the hero of Chalmette. Also a specific name was needed for the growing suburb. It was about this time that the Marquis de la Fayette made his memorable tour of the United States, and, in particular, a visit to Louisiana. What greater honor could this section of that former French territory pay to one of its great heroes than the adoption of his name as its own? Hence, there was another new faubourg above the City of New Orleans, Faubourg Lafayette.

C. Pollock Notarian Records
G. King's Creole Families of New Orleans

APPENDIX

As Carondelet made ready to leave New Orleans he thought it proper to award Don Pedro Rousseau a citation.

CITATION

DON FRANCESCO LUIS HECTOR, Baron de Carondelet, Knight of the Order of St. John, Field Marshall of the Royal Armies, Commander General, Royal Vice-Patron of the Provinces of West Florida and Louisiana, Inspector of the Veteran Troops and Militia of the said provinces:—

> I certify that Lieutenant Colonel Don Pedro Rousseau has added to the particular and meritorious services which he rendered during the past war against England as commander of the brig Galveston, his services in the river as commander of the Galleys Fleet, not only on the diverse places which he considered necessary for the defense of the river during the war against France, but also in the attack and establishment of the Fort San Fernando de las Barrancas in the country of the Chicachas Indians and in the naval station of the Ohio, in the upper Louisiana, in all of which deeds he has shown great zeal in the service of His Majesty, as well as activity and courage, all of which I make known in this letter, signed by my own hand and sealed with my coat of arms, and countersigned by the honorary Secretary and Commissioner of War of His Majesty's Government, in New Orleans the fifth day of August of 1797.

El Baron de Carondelet

By hand of His Lordship
Andres Lopez Armesto

When, on April 29, 1795, some Indians aided by General Robertson were marching toward Barràncas de Margot, Tomas Portelle, commandant at New Madrid, wrote to Rousseau, May 4, 1795.

"Yesterday, the third of the current month, under oath, I received from a citizen of this post named Estans (Easton) the following declaration:

> "He told me that he had left some thirty Chicacha Indians at the mouth of the Cumberland River who were accompanied by fifteen white men whose destination was the same, who were armed with carbines; and in the same district where they were, was a certain number

of white men (a numerous party) likewise armed, who were about to go to that place where Your Grace is, under the pretext of aiding the Indians of the Creeks. . . . I shall do whatever possible if they arrive at this post to prevent the white men from passing; but if they persist in it, I shall allow them to continue their voyage, in accordance with the orders I have received to have pursued by boat or boats of his Majesty that are found there . . . I advise Your Grace of this, so that in case it falls out according to my orders, and I assure you that as the above mentioned men arrive at this destination, I shall immediately dispatch a pirogue advising you of what they determine to do, so that Your Grace may be able to act in consequence of that determination.

"May God preserve Your Grace many years, etc.
                                        Portelle

"Addressed: Don Pedro Rousseau, Commander of the Galleys of the Mississippi
"Countersigned as an enclosure (i.e., a copy) to Duke de la Alcudia"

Nicholas Rousseau

Nicholas Rousseau, a younger brother of Pierre George, was born on June 14, 1752 at La Tremblade, France. He came to America with his father as a child. While there is no available information concerning where his father settled when he first came to this country, it is known that he established residence in New Orleans in 1764, and placed his children in a private school where they were educated in English as well as in French. At the beginning of the American Revolution Nicholas enlisted in the Continental navy, and was promoted to the rank of lieutenant.

After the end of the Revolution he continued to serve with the same rank in the army of Galvez, and was stationed for a time at Natchitoches while his brother, Pierre George, was commandant there.

He married Marie Gradenigo, whose father, John Gradenigo, was a nephew of the Very Rev. Giovanni Gradenigo, whose father, John Gradenigo, was a nephew of the Very Rev. Giovanni Gradenigo, Bishop (doge of

Venice), descended from the ancient Venetian family of Doge Pietro Gradenigo, who drove Bajamonte Tiepolo and the Quirini family from Venice when they attempted to seize the Piazza in 1310.

There is no clear record of why the powerful Giovanni Gradenigo's nephew migrated to Louisiana but it was rumored that they disagreed and parted. The doge was very wealthy, having an estate valued at around eighty million dollars. And although he was not on good terms with his nephew he made a will leaving one-third of his vast estate to the Holy Roman Catholic Church, one-third to a nephew in Florence, Italy, and one-third to his nephew, John Gradenigo, who resided in Opelousas, Louisiana.

John Gradenigo died in 1809 without making a claim for his share in the estate, which was held by the Italian government "until legally claimed according to said will." But his descendants, among the best families of the Teche country and New Orleans (especially the old and prominent Voorhies family), tried for many years to establish the claim, without success.

Nicholas Rousseau died on March 6, 1824, and was buried in the cemetery of the Parish of St. Louis, New Orleans. He left several children. Among them was Eulalie Rousseau, born March 2, 1788, who married August Dupré, son of Jacques Dupré, governor of Louisiana (1830-31). One of his granddaughters, Zilia Rousseau, married Alexandre Mouton, governor of Louisiana (1843-46). While residing in Washington with her husband (then) Senator Mouton, the celebrated sculptor, Powers, carved the "Greek Slave." In selecting a model hand for his famous statue he is said to have chosen the hand of Zilia, who was noted alike for the beauty of her face and the symmetry of her form. Her hand was used also as a model for the hand of Pocahontas in the painting of that Indian princess which hangs in the rotunda of the Capitol in Washington.

There are many descendants of Nicholas Rousseau among the first families of the Teche country and New Orleans.

Excerpts from Letters

Carondelet says in a letter addressed to Don Luis de las Cases, April 7, 1794:

Until we know with certainty the part which will be taken by General Clark who gives himself the showy title of Mariscal de Campo (i.e., Field Marshall) of the French armies and of the revolutionary Legions of the Mississippi, the squadron of the galleys will remain in Nuevo Madrid, where, according to the information which I have received from their commander, Don Pedro Rousseau, it will arrive at the end of this month, ready to attack the enemy as they leave the Ohio, whenever it can be done with decided advantage, or to keep them from passing Las Barrancas a Margot forty leagues below, if our savages promise to aid it during the action from land, and with the advantage that the river furnishes them, which absolutely commands the passage; lastly to fight on retiring, without engaging in doubtful action until uniting with the two other galleys which are below the forts of Nogales, in case that the savages return to our opponants, as they have done several times, the last time being in the conquest of Penzacola, in regard to the English, their allies.

NOTES FROM HOUCK'S HISTORY OF MISSOURI
and Spanish Regime in Missouri
Page 121 — Portell's letter to Rousseau

1795 - May 1—

Yesterday, the third of the current month, under oath, I received from a citizen of this post named Estans the following declaration:

He told me that he had left some thirty Chicaha Indians at the mouth of the Cumberland River who were accompanied by fifteen white men whose destination was the same, who were armed with carbines; and in the same district where they were, there was a certain number of white men (a more numerous party) likewise armed, who were about to go to that place where Your Grace, is under pretext of aiding the Indians of the above-mentioned nation in their war against the Creeks.

I shall do whatever is possible if they arrive at this post to prevent the whites from passing; but if they persist in it, I shall allow them to continue their voyage, in accordance with the orders I have received to have them pursued by the boat or boats of His Majesty that are found there.

I advise Your Grace of this, so that in case it falls out according to my orders, and I assure you as soon as the above-mentioned men arrive at this destination, I shall immediately despatch a pirouge advising you of what they determine to do, so that Your Grace may be able to act in consequence of that determination.

May God preserve Your Grace for many years.

Thomas Portell

Addressed: "Pedro Rousseau, Commandant of the galleys"
Countersigned as an enclosure to Duke de la Alcudia:

"Baron de Carondelet"

Sons of Pierre George Rousseau and Catherine Wiltz Milhet
COMMODORE LAWRENCE ROUSSEAU

Lawrence Rousseau was born in September, 1790, and after serving some years as an officer in the United States Navy was promoted to the rank of captain on March 3, 1837. His commission was signed by President Andrew Jackson. The original document is now in the hands of Mrs. Edwin X .de Verges of New Orleans, who is a great niece of his wife. In 1838 he was designated to examine and make a survey of the coast from Key West to the Sabine River, and to establish a suitable lighthouse service. He completed this survey in November of the same year. He was later placed in command of the Macedonian, which served as the flagship for Commodore W. B. Shubrick. In 1843 he established the Navy Yard at Memphis, Tennessee; and in 1848 he established the Naval Station at New Orleans, and made "a conditional contract with Mr. J. B. Dupieru (Dupeyre) for a piece of ground, in area about 25 acres, on the right bank of the River, situated about one and one-half miles from the ferry landing between the City and the town of Algiers, for a price of fifteen thousand dollars." On October 22, 1845 he was appointed as commanding officer of the U.S. Squadron on the Brazil Station with the USS Columbia as his flagship. On October 11, 1847, he requested, in a letter written from Hampton Roads, leave of absence from his duties as commanding officer of the U.S. Squadron on the Brazil

135

Station, because "important business requires my presence in New Orleans by the 1st of November." On October 13, 1847, John Y. Mason, Secretary of the Navy, congratulated him on his safe return to the United States, "after an arduous and honorable service in an important and highly responsible command." On May 4, 1854, he was ordered to command the Navy Yard at Pensacola, Florida, where he remained until April 29, 1857, when he returned to New Orleans and was placed on waiting orders. On February 1, 1861, he resigned from the U.S. Navy, and the DAILY DELTA carried the following editorial:

"We learn that this estimable and excellent officer has thrown up his commission in the United States Navy. Com. Rousseau is one of those whom the Southern Confederacy would require immediately in the organization of the navy, and his numerous friends as well as the well-wishers of the South will be glad to know that, by resigning from a position which might have brought him into collision with his native State, he has placed it in his power immediately to tender his services to that section which all the associations of his birth and life have made dear to him.

"Com. Rousseau was born in this city at the close of the last century, and entered the Navy as acting mid-ship-man, if our recollection is correct, in 1807 or 1808, during the administration of President Jefferson. He was one of those who gallantly fought in defense of their country through the War of 1812, and served in several engagements on the Lakes during the memorable conflict. He was always considered as a most active and trustworthy officer, and commanded universal respect by his decisions of character and personal courage—qualities calculated to make him reverenced and beloved by all who served under him, and esteemed worthy of commands of danger and delicacy by his superior officers. In 1845, when questions of great importance were pending between the Brazilian Government and our own, Henry A. Wise was sent as our minister plenipotentiary, and Commodore Rousseau was instructed with the command of the squadron. This post he likewise filled with honor to himself and to his country. After a few years of rest, Commodore Rousseau was appointed to the Pensacola Navy Yard, where he had already been stationed on previous occasions, and where he remained until 1857. He then returned to New Orleans, and has since been awaiting orders.

"A faithful Louisianian, one whose interest and sympathy have ever been linked with his native State, he now resigns, and places himself at the disposal of Louisiana, or whatever confederacy she may unite herself with. Such officers as Commodore Rousseau will not be forgotten when the organization of the navy is considered, for the protection of our commercial interests and national honor."

Admiral Raphael Semmes said in his book, MEMOIRS OF SERVICE AFLOAT: "I arrived in New Orleans on Monday, April 22, and at once put myself in communication with the commanding officer, the venerable Lawrence Rousseau, since gone to his long home, full of years and full of honors, like a true son of the South he had obeyed the first call of his fatherland, the State of Louisiana, and tore off the seal from the commission of a federal Captain, which he had honored for forty years. I will not say 'peace to his ashes,' for the spirit of a christian gentleman, which animated his frame during life, has doubtless received its appropriate reward; nor will I say aught of his name, or fame, for these are emblemed in the memories of his countrymen. He was my friend, and in that name 'friend' I pronounce his eulogy."

During the Civil War Lawrence Rousseau was Chief of the Office of Detail and Equipment. . . He was seventy-one at the beginning of the War but still full of energy. He was stationed at Richmond, Va.; Savannah, Ga.; Jackson, Mississippi; Selma, Alabama, and toward the end of the war at the vital station of Mobile, Alabama.

NOTE: In the letters and documents which I have gathered for this book I have found names and places spelled in various ways, and have not changed or attempted to correct them. For instance. Thomas Portell is in some documents PORTEL, in others PORTELLE. Apalache is in some records APALACHEE, APALACHIE. There are other similar instances.

Gustave Sebastian Rousseau

Gustave Sebastian Rousseau was born July 11, 1806, at New Orleans. He was admitted to West Point on July 1, 1824, and graduated therefrom on July 1, 1828. From 1830 to 1833 he was stationed at Jefferson Barracks in St. Louis with Jefferson Davis, Sidney Johnson, Robert E. Lee and others. While in St. Louis he married Emily Lee, who was a grand-daughter of Dr. Andre A. Conde, of Aunis, France; he had been Post Surgeon at Fort Chartres in Illinois, and moved to St. Louis with St. Ange de Bellerive in 1765. He had married at Mobile, in 1763, Marie Ann de la Ferne, daughter of Pierre Ignace de la Ferne, a "Chirurgien Major pour le Roy at Nouvelle Chartres, Mobile." Her father, Patrick Lee, was the son of Thomas Lee who had much correspondence with Governor O'Reilly of Louisiana in regard to trade practices, and whose letters are preserved in the archives of Seville, Spain. In 1833 Gustave Sebastian Rousseau resigned from the U.S. Army and went to New Orleans with his wife, and became cashier of the Union Bank. He later resided on Victoria Plantation at Bayou Goula, Louisiana, which he purchased. Shortly after this he was appointed Brigadier General, Louisiana Militia. Meantime he had taken up the study of law, and was a practicing attorney in the town of Plaquemine in Iberville parish. While serving as Brigadier General, Louisiana Militia (1846-1855) the War with Mexico broke out and he led the Louisiana Tigers to the Mexican border. His call for volunteers (issued from his HEADQUARTERS, 8th BRIGADE, L.M., Plaquemine, La., May 4, 1846) appeared in the Baton Rouge Gazette on May 8, 1846, and did not go unheeded, for on May 13, 1846, the following appeared in the Daily Delta, published in New Orleans:

"When we speak of military movements now we know not where to begin or where to end. For such is the ardor—such is the excitement that pervades the city that little in the way of detail can be gathered. The influx of volunteers from the country continues to increase. Hour after hour bands of these brave spirits pass our office. . . Of those who arrived yesterday, one were a company from Iberville, under the command of General G.S. Rousseau."

Associated with him were Captain William H. Higgins, 1st Lieutenant Gustave Lauve, and several second lieutenants.

When General Rousseau returned from the Mexican War he remained at the head of the Louisiana Militia until 1855, and again took up the practice of law in the town of Plaquemine. He died on January 29, 1879. He was driving a gig, as usual from his law office to his plantation when an old Negro stopped him and begged some tobacco. As he stopped and handed the Negro the tobacco he fell forward and died instantly.

Other sons of Pierre George Rousseau, who did not enter the military field, were practicing lawyers in New Orleans:

Pierre Andre Rousseau (whose residence was at 154 Barracks Street) was an attorney, and also U.S. Inspector of Revenue.

Rodolphe Rousseau (whose residence was at 71 Bayou Road) was an attorney. His office was in St. Anthony Square.

Octave Sebastian Rousseau was a judge in St. Bernard Parish.

Emanuel Gayoso de Lemos left a son, Férnando de Lemos, who married Lodoiska Ceilla Perez, daughter of Helene Toutant Beauregard and Don Emmanuel Perez, who served as commandant at Baton Rouge during the Spanish regime in Louisiana. From this marriage there was a daughter, Felicite Gayoso de Lemos, who married Charles Tennent, a merchant of Houma, La. They had two daughters, Marie Perez, and Jeanne Lodoiska, and a son, Fernando Gayoso de Lemos. Jeanne Lodoiska Tennent married Robert Barrow, and they had four daughters: Miss Irene Barrow, Mrs. O. Topping, Mrs. Harris Dawson, and Mrs. Grenes Cole.

Genealogy
of
Pierre Georges Rousseau
CIRCA 1678 TO 1964

All available research on the Genealogy of Pierre Georges Rousseau reaches as far back as circa 1678.

Records of the Parish Church at La Tremblade, Saintonge, (now Charente Maritime) France, reveal that Pierre George Rousseau was born and baptized on June 3, 1751, the fourth child of Marine Captain Sieur Pierre Rousseau and Marie Eustelle Daniaud.

Further research was made by Madame, Veuve, Helene Rousseau Forgit of La Tremblade and Angouleme, France, during November of 1963. In the archives of the Parish Church, now deposited in the City Hall at La Tremblade, Madame Forgit found that the Rousseau families were living in La Tremblade as early as 1678. In 1738 there were three Rousseau families domiciled there: Sieur Pierre Rousseau, married to Marie Eustelle Daniaud, Joseph Rousseau, Royal Notary, and Michel Rousseau. Mrs. Rousseau Forgit remarks that "They probably belonged to the same family, since at that time the families remained in their village."

From the records covering the years 1738 through 1770 Madame Forgit found that to Sieur Pierre Rousseau and Marie Eustelle Daniaud were born six children, three girls and three boys. These were, as copied from the record:

MARIE - MAGDELEINE, daughter of Pierre Rousseau, marine officer, and of Eustelle Daniaud, born and baptized October 31, 1744.

PIERRE, son of Pierre Rousseau and of Marie Eustelle Daniaud, baptized privately at the home because of danger of death, on February 28, 1747. Buried in the cemetery of La Tremblade on March 2, 1747.

ELIZABETH, daughter of Captain Pierre Rousseau and Marie Eustelle Daniaud, born and baptized on August 29, 1749.

PIERRE GEORGES, son of Pierre Rousseau, Marine Captain, and of Marie Eustelle Daniaud, born and baptized on June 3, 1751.

NICHOLAS PIERRE, son of Pierre Rousseau, Marine Captain, and of Marie Eustelle Daniaud, born on June 14, 1752, baptized on June 15.

MARIE ANNE, daughter of Pierre Rousseau, Marine Officer, and of Marie Eustelle Daniaud, born on January 18, 1754, baptized on the 20th.

Sieur Pierre Rousseau and his two sons, Pierre Georges and Nicolas Pierre, emigrated to America.

Pierre Georges Rousseau married Catherine Milhet, August 28, 1783. Catherine was the daughter of Margarethe Wiltz and Joseph Milhet. To this union were born twelve children:

1. MARIE ANASTASIE HORTENSE ROUSSEAU
   b.
   m. John Baptiste Soraparu, October 9, 1799
   d. August 19, 1845
      Their children:
      1. ZOE SORAPARU
         b. March, 1810
         m. Edward H. Hedge
         d. March 10, 1837
            Their issue:
            MARY HEDGE
            b. August 5, 1836
            Never married
            d. Nov. 23, 1912

      2. JOHN BAPTISTE SORAPARU
         b.
         m. Marie Laheville of St. Esprite, France
         d. Sept. 19, 1892
            Their issue:
            LOUIS SORAPARU
            b. Jan. 9, 1845
            never married
            d. 1924

2. PIERRE ANDRE ANTOINE ROUSSEAU
   b. Dec. 5, 1787
   m. Marie Felicite Laure Dreux 1815 (b. in 1801, d. Feb. 4, 1886). She was the daughter of Guy Charles Dreux by his second marriage to Felicite Crudeaux.

   d. Jan. 14, 1840
      Their issue:
      1. PIERRE LOUIS ALFRED ROUSSEAU
         b. Feb. 5, 1820, baptized March 13, 1820
         m.
         d.
         (His birth certificate in possession of John Alfred [J. Alf.] Rousseau.)

      2. MARGUERITE ROUSSEAU
         b. 1816
         m. Charles M. Carriere
         d. Oct. 7, 1854

Their children:

(1) Alphonse C. Carriere and (2) Albert Carriere
(never married)

3. ALFRED L. ROUSSEAU
   b. 1822 ?
   m. Widow Theresa Teitenberg, Jan. 4, 1859. She was born
      1837 in Westphalia, Prussia, the daughter of Christian
   d. May 17, 1888

   Their issue, two children:

   (1) Emilie Rousseau
       d. 1920
       m. Arthur C. de La Marre, July 22,1882

   (2) Alfred Lawrence Rousseau
       b. 1867
       m. Eugenie Leonie Rantz, who died Oct. 19, 1954,
                                           age 86 yrs.
       d. by drowning 1909, age 42 yrs.

       Their issue, three children:

       1. John Alfred (J. Alf.) Rousseau
          b. April 3, 1887
          m. Frances Gaudance Links, Aug. 27, 1924

       2. August Rousseau
          b. 1889
          d. 1893
          Eugenie Therese Rousseau

3. LAWRENCE ROUSSEAU
   b. 1790
   m. Josephine de Lino Cruzat, Feb. 18, 1819 (b. May 12, 1800;
   d. Sept. 4, 1866   d. Aug. 22, 1878)
   no children

4. FELIPPA ROUSSEAU
   b.
   m. Alexander Hamilton Smith
   d.

   Their issue:

   1. Adelaide Lydia Smith
      b.
      m. Col. Samuel Wegmann
      m. John W. Hardie

      Their child:
      Mary Josephine Hardie
      b.
      d. at Hotel Dieu

2. Gilbert Smith
b.
never married
d. prior to 1892

3. Marie Josephine Smith
b.
m. Maurice Willard
d.

4. Hamilton Smith
b.
never married

5. JOSEPHINE ROUSSEAU
b. March, 1796
m. Louis Lauret
d.

Their child:
Nicida Lauret
b.
m. Pierre Jorda

Their children:
Octavie Jorda, who married Charles Baquie
Lucie Jorda, who married J. C. Phillipi, died Oct. 13, 1917
Nisida Jorda, who married Herman Kahle
Emile Jorda, who married Adele Lamothe
Felicie Jorda, in religion

6. ADELE ROUSSEAU
b. October, 1797
never married
d. October 23, 1818

7. JOHN BAPTISTE ROUSSEAU
b.
never married
d. drowned in 1815 while serving as a midshipman in U. S. Navy

8. RODOLPHE ROUSSEAU (He was a Judge in St. Bernard Parish,
b. Feb., 1802   La.)
m. Sarah McDougal Murphy, June 14, 1830
d. August 20, 1862
no children

9. ETIENNE ROUSSEAU
b.
m. Marie Emilie Huchet de Kernion, August 27, 1831. She was the
daughter of Pierre Huchet de Kernion and Marie Genevieve
Clara Coulon Jumonville de Villier.

Their children:

Claire Emilie Rousseau, who married Victor Garidel
Marie Charlotte Claire Rousseau
Marie Stephanie Rousseau
Marie Aimie Rousseau

10. OCTAVE SEBASTIAN ROUSSEAU
    b. July 11, 1806
    never married
    d. April 29, 1866

11. GUSTAVE SEBASTIAN ROUSSEAU, twin of above
    b. July 11, 1806
    m. Emily Lee, June 28, 1830
       (He was a General in the U. S. Army)
    d. January 29, 1879

    Their children:

    1. Octave Sebastian Rousseau
       b. 1855
       never married
       d. Feb. 20, 1907

    2. Josephine Rousseau
       b. 1833
       never married
       d.

    3. Sarah Rousseau
       b.
       m. Joachim Martinez (b. March 29, 1830; d. Dec. 9, 1874)
       d. 1883

       Their children:
       (1) Albert Joseph Martinez
           b. Sept. 22, 1865; d. April 14, 1956
              m. Olivia Marionneaux, Dec. 18, 1888 (b. Sept. 15,
                                                   1871; d. June 2, 1950)
       (2) Gustave Sebastian Martinez
           b. Oct. 21, 1870
              m. Bertha E. Achee, April 23, 1896
              d. June 18, 1932

       (3) Lelia Martinez
           b. December 8, 1867
              m. Philip Landry
           d. September 12, 1914

       (4) Adele Martinez
           b. Oct. 5, 1874
              m. Charles Dupuy, Sept. 7, 1892
           d. April 22, 1961

12. AIMIE AMELINE ROUSSEAU
    b. December, 1808
    never married
    d.

Bibliography

Spain in the Mississippi Valley — Lawrence Kinnaird

Louis Houck's History of Missouri

Louis Houck's The Spanish Regime in Missouri

A Naval History of the American Revolution — Gardener W. Allen

The New York Public Library

The National Archives, Washington, D.C.

Missouri Historical Society

Department of the Navy, Washington, D.C.

Navy Dept. Office of Naval Records and Library

The Library of Congress

Standard History of New Orleans, Henry Rightor

History of Louisiana, Charles Gayarré

Grace King's History of Louisiana

The Archives de la Charente-Maritime, la Tremblade, France

The Gazette, New Orleans

The Courier, New Orleans

Pictorial History of Pensacola, City of Five Flags, John W. Cole

Times-Democrat, Henry C. Castellanos (The Siege of Pensacola and the Story of Pierre Rousseau).

Howard-Tilton Memorial Library, New Orleans

The Louisiana Historical Quarterly

Francois X. Martin's History of Louisiana.

INDEX

INDEX (continued)

INDEX (continued)

www.ingramcontent.com/pod-product-compliance
Lightning Source LLC
LaVergne TN
LVHW011237080426
835509LV00005B/533